# Thirteen Reasons

## Not to Join the Mormon Church

Donny Harris

ISBN: 1493645870
ISBN 13: 9781493645879
Library of Congress Control Number: 2013920776
CreateSpace Independent Publishing Platform
North Charleston, South Carolina

# $\mathcal{F}$OREWORD

## Thirteen Reasons

## By Donny Harris

WHILE GROWING UP a member of the Mormon faith, I did not realize at the time that many people do not know "Mormon church" is not the church's official name. The official name is actually The Church of Jesus Christ of Latter-day Saints, or simply, the LDS church.

Throughout this book I will refer to the Church of Jesus Christ of Latter-day Saints, its members, and its beliefs using the term "Mormon." Using this term is not considered a derogatory reference toward them. In fact, members of the Mormon faith take no offense to this term. Actually, most members of the Mormon church will identify themselves in this very way: "I'm a member of The Church of Jesus Christ of Latter-day Saints…I'm a Mormon."

While it is true that I was raised in the Mormon faith, I am not writing this book about my life. Rather, this book is about the basic beliefs of the Mormon church as stated in the Thirteen Articles of Faith, a statement of faith penned by founding leader, Joseph Smith Jr., and how those beliefs differ from biblical Christianity as a whole. I mention a few of my own experiences here, merely for the purpose of illustration.

I have seen a great shift in outreach tactics over the years and have noticed a clear attempt by the Mormon church to appear more traditional and biblical in its approach to outreach. Unfortunately, this new approach is only outward, as the teachings that separate them from biblical Christianity are still well intact.

For example, when I was a kid, we often visited the temple grounds visitor center in Salt Lake City, Utah. In this center, visitors are introduced to basic fundamentals of the Mormon faith and are introduced to Joseph Smith's claims of how he received the "Golden Plates" (from which he claims to have gotten the Book of Mormon). Visitors also learn how the Mormon church came to be known by its members as the only true church on earth.

I grew up in Salt Lake City, and my family would often visit the grounds as a faith-building family outing. In our visits, I loved the visitor center and all the stories about Joseph Smith, the golden plates, American Indians, pioneers trekking out west, and such. I recently returned after many years of being away from Utah, and I was shocked at what I saw.

Rather than being up front about their true beliefs as they once were, the church now begins the tour by talking about and quoting verses from the Bible.

As the tour begins no traces of these once prominent teachings are seen. Nothing about the Book of Mormon, Joseph Smith, nor any of the other teachings unique to Mormonism are visible. A visitor moving from the ground level to the upper floor encounters an inspiring statute of Jesus, and a sweet-sounding voice quotes a verse that Jesus spoke from the Bible. If one were simply to visit the ground and upper floor of the visitor center, they could easily leave thinking that the Mormons are just another misunderstood Christian sect. In fact, one of my Christian friends who went with me to see the center said "So far, I don't see anything presented that isn't just a normal, typical Christian belief." It wasn't until we ventured into the lower level of the center that we began to hear some of those other things that fall outside of the traditional, biblical, Christian teachings.

It didn't dawn on me at the time; only later at home did I realize just how metaphorically this new layout could describe their whole new approach to outreach.

Rather than coming straight out and telling people how different their beliefs are from true doctrine, as they once did, they attempt to first show how similar they are. In this way, they hide (as it were) the lower levels of their true beliefs under layers of biblical smoke screen. I say this because underneath this facade, the beliefs have not changed, only the outreach tactics. Truly, if these changes were a result of a newfound awareness of the truth of the Word of God and its importance, it would be great. I assure you, however, that nothing has changed except on the surface.

I find it vital to explain the differences between the terms they have borrowed from biblical Christianity and the actual doctrine behind them. These terms sound very Christian and must be clarified in order to avoid deception.

Throughout my upbringing, I was given tools to defend the Mormon faith, as well as Christianity as I knew it. For each possible point a Christian would raise about the Bible, we were given a good comeback. When I heard a member talking about how someone had questioned their faith or made statements that the church was not true, it was common for us to comfort each other with these comebacks. If, for instance our faith was being challenged, we would often say, "We should expect this persecution because we are merely suffering the persecution Christ predicted would come to all true believers." Every time we were questioned or someone spoke out against us, it was considered persecution against us, and thus couldn't possibly be the truth. This "persecution complex," as I will call it, was the hiding place to which many of us would run if our faith was being questioned.

I see this complex in action when I read statements online regarding anti-Mormon books. When church members see a statement that conflicts with their understanding of truth, they will say something like "Why does everyone harass the Mormons and our faith?" Most Mormons are so convinced they have found "the only true church on earth," that any challenge to this idea is received as harassment. It's not that I don't understand how they could feel this way, as I felt the same way in my day—I said the same things. If fact, it only made me feel more correct and strong in the faith if someone challenged my beliefs because, as we would say, "Christ said we would be persecuted and hated for the faith. So rejoice and be glad when it happens because they also persecuted the prophets who were before us."

Only now that I have been set free of these things am I able to see that if someone tells us the truth, no matter how hard that truth may be to receive, it is not persecution but actually the most loving act one can do. Please understand that one doesn't have to know that they are in deception for it to be a reality.

The truth may contradict a feeling you once experienced or even everything you have held so dearly all your life as from God. Friend, please hear me as I promise you that if you are truly seeking for answers and if you are willing to follow the truth and to please God rather than mankind, you will find the truth you are looking for. You must be willing to choose God over your family, friends, spouse, even your own personal feelings. Our feelings can deceive us, but the truth will not.

May the Spirit of God and His Word alone influence your decision, with or without anything I have to say. I'm not claiming to be anyone special. I'm just another undeserving man who has been set free from the fear of death and hell by the grace of God. I boldly approach the throne of God's grace daily with no shame, even though I am still wholly unworthy of His love and mercy. Because of this freedom I received through faith in the Word of God, the Bible—a freedom the Mormon faith never provided— it is now my greatest joy in life to help others, and even hopefully you, to also live in this unmerited peace and hope as well.

# Chapter 1

## God's Word

*I* MET A man who said he investigated counterfeit money for a living. I admit I do not know anything about this work or if he was even telling the truth, but his comments changed my life.

I asked, "How many different types of counterfeit bills are out there?"

Smiling, he simply said, "Quite a few."

In my ignorance, I exclaimed, "Wow, you must need to study many types of counterfeit bills in order to recognize which ones are fakes."

He said "Not at all. We just know what the real ones look like. Once you know how the real thing looks, you can spot a counterfeit a mile away."

---

I HAVE MANY happy childhood memories of my days in the Church of Jesus Christ of Latter-day Saints. I went on scout trips, outings with the elders, and I sang in the choir. I have also had the wonderful experience of singing in the tabernacle on the temple grounds in Salt Lake City. I was ordained an elder and was "sealed" in the temple to my wife.

I've always enjoyed the sweet nature of the wonderful Mormon people I have met throughout my life. My reason for writing this book is not to belittle anyone's faith. I have no complaint about mistreatment by leadership. I don't claim any of the common reasons I've heard others use to discredit "The Church" when they no longer want to be a part of it.

Instead, my purpose for writing is to share with my dear family and friends the reasons that I have completely separated myself from the teachings of the Mormon church. I want all who will listen to know that, whereas I never received the peace and victory over sin that was promised to me by following the teachings of the Mormon faith, I now have been given great peace and victory by following the teachings of the Bible alone.

If my family were to ask me the reason that I have no desire to return to the Mormon church, I would say that there are at least thirteen reasons. They are called the Thirteen Articles of Faith. I hope you will prayerfully hear out what I have to say with an open heart, and I will tell you why.

In my search for truth, I haven't felt the need to read what others have written about the Mormon church and the problems with its theology. I have, instead, become an avid student of the Bible. Studying the Bible with the help of the Holy Spirit gave me all the tools I needed to find the truth.

I never bothered to fully read any of the books I had seen denouncing the Mormon church because I couldn't understand why none of these books seemed directed to those actually in the faith. I'm sure there are some, but I didn't see any. As a Mormon, I often asked myself who those books were written for. They were obviously not for the lifelong Mormon struggling with his or her faith. Mormons know when their faith is not being represented in a true light.

It also bothered me that those books seemed to be so full of disdain over the subject that compassion toward the people was not evident. I know firsthand that these are wonderful people who are only trying to follow their convictions to the best of their ability. They are not some band of mindless fools as many have portrayed them to be.

While a member of the church, I found myself asking on several occasions, if the Mormon church was not the "only true church on the face of the earth," why does it take lies to discredit it. Well, I have come to see that it doesn't. Please bear with me and my unrefined writing skills, and I will show you why.

## My Deliverance, My Peace

I have prayerfully decided to write this book in defense of the most amazing book ever written and compiled—the Bible. While often misquoted, misunderstood, neglected, and tossed to the side, this holy book has withstood the test of time and the scrutiny of the wisest atheist scholars.

## The Latent Deception

From my earliest memories I can now see that it has always been the church's unspoken aim to shift attention away from the Bible and toward the Book of Mormon. If their claims were true, why wouldn't they? Believers are handed a Book of Mormon and told it is the Word of God. Then they are handed a Bible and told that it is the Word of God—*only as far as it is translated correctly*. I have come to realize that what they mean, in reality, is that only the parts of the Bible that seem to agree with the Mormon theologies and the Book of Mormon are true.

The assumption seems clear: you'd be unwise to pay more attention to something that's only partially true than to the full truth, wouldn't you? So, while many Mormons naturally read both books, they give more heed to the Book of Mormon.

The possible meanings of key verses in the Bible are so well ingrained in the members as to make it almost impossible for them to come to any other conclusion to a passage than the one they have been instructed to believe. I decided, however, to take a different approach to study than the way I was taught. Rather than picking verses here and there in order to prove a doctrinal claim someone has made (or even an idea I already possessed), I simply search any topic cover to cover to see what the Bible said about the topic over all. Knowing that God cannot contradict Himself, I looked to the Bible alone—not someone's rendering of it—to teach me. I found that these supposed "missing elements" of the Bible were beautifully concealed as a piece of gold in a field. In order to find them, I had to dig them out. I could not take a verse merely on surface value but had to weigh it out with everything else that has already been written on the same subject. Only then could I "rightly divide the Word of God."

For example, if Paul in one place says emphatically that it is by grace alone we are saved, not of works, yet James says that faith without works is dead, I can know for certain—because God is neither a liar nor a deceiver—that if two ideas seem in opposition, then it is my understanding that is in conflict, not the Word of God.

There is a balancing effect that is seen throughout the Word of God, wherein the Lord says on one hand that we are to "keep the Sabbath day holy"; but on the other hand that it is okay to "do good" work on the Sabbath. So we must ask ourselves if God has changed His mind or if is there a bigger lesson here than just the hard-and-fast, do-or-die of the law.

Often, when I found verses that seemed hard to grasp, the very key to understanding was found in two or more places in the Bible. I found that every major point necessary for salvation followed this God-given rule. So, it is especially dangerous to interpret any one verse to mean something that must contradict everything else the Bible already says on the same subject in order to be true.

In fact, I can't think of an example where a major salvation point is only found in one spot. The Bible says by the mouth of two or three witnesses shall every word be established. I found this to hold true. I found that verses often cited as flaws are more accurately called mysteries. That's right, we don't have all the answers, nor will we in this life. By design, there are things that will not be known until Christ returns and sets up His kingdom. Why would God do this? Because, as the Lord says in the Bible, when the end comes and all He has promised does come about, we will know that, all along, God was with us. We will see, as will the wicked who rejected Him, that His ways were plainly before us the whole time in His Word. We will clearly see that the wicked were without excuse. We will understand that God wanted to be found by each of us, but that we had to look for ourselves in order to find the truth in Him and His Word.

## God is able to keep His Word intact.

For many years, the dealings of God toward mankind were handed down from generation to generation without the benefit of written testimonies. Despite this fact, God was able to preserve His Word. Skipping forward in history, we find Moses, a (most likely) highly educated man from Egypt, called of God to make a written record of the words and laws of God. Still later in time, we find the apostles' records of the life and ministry of Christ. After the gospel was proclaimed and the apostles all passed away, records from many sources came together in remarkable agreement to form the Bible we have today. Please consider, friend, that God is more than able to protect His Word.

An often-cited teaching by Mormons is that Christ predicted a "falling away" would happen before His return. This falling away, however, was of the church at large and mankind, not God's Word and not all believers.

Consider the great prophet Elijah, who felt that he was the only true believer left on earth. However, God had reserved unto Himself, seven thousand men that had not bowed to Baal (1 Kings 19:18).

When it looks to mankind that all is lost, the Lord Himself is able to preserve the truth of His Word. The Word of God has remained intact from the beginning and will continue for all time.

## Truth is not subject to what we believe or our spiritual feelings.

At each fasting and testimony meeting at the first of the month, we would declare, "I believe that Joseph Smith was a true prophet, I believe the Book of Mormon is the word of God..." Please understand, friend, that truth is not subject to our burning bosoms, our understanding, or our feelings. The truth of God is not a feeling, it's the truth. When a spirit or a burning bosom agrees with the Word of God, it is truth. When it doesn't, it's a lie.

To illustrate what I mean about truth, please consider this: the best thinkers of mankind once wholeheartedly believed the world was flat. They believed this with all their heart. They taught it in school, church, everywhere with great force. But this strong belief was powerless to change the actual truth. The truth was not relative to their personal convictions. It wasn't subject to heavy handed church leaders or the paradigm of the day. The truth was among them the whole time, they just didn't understand it. The truth of this subject was right there in the Bible the whole time. The Bible has called earth round for thousands of years.

Consider the words of Isaiah 40:22. "It is he that sitteth upon the circle of the earth, and the inhabitants thereof are as grasshoppers; that stretcheth out the heavens as a curtain, and spreadeth them out as a tent to dwell in." Why didn't they see this? The Bible is only understood by inspiration of God, not by man's wisdom. This is why people see what they want to see in the Bible. The Lord Himself has designed His Word in such a way that only the true seeker will find the truth. Due to unbelief God degreed: "And he said go, and tell this people, hear ye indeed, but understand not, and see ye indeed, but perceive not" (Isaiah 6:9).

In Isaiah 11:12, for example, some say that Isaiah taught the world was flat simply because he metaphorically used the term "four corners of the earth." This is simply ridiculous, as we still use this phrase to this very day when talking about the four directions of the compass.

Or consider a modern day example of the same type of error occurring in our day. Those who altogether deny the existence of God and choose to believe in the so-called big bang theory. They simply choose, without proof, to believe that everything just sprang into existence from nothing by mere chance.

If you are honest, you can see it takes more faith to believe matter just formed on its own from nothing, collected, then exploded; than that a God created it. Any elementary science teacher could tell you that you must first have matter, gasses, and an energy source in order to have anything to collect or explode. Yet they unapologetically, arrogantly, and ignorantly cling to completely unprovable fables, simply because it gives them some vague thing to hold on to in order to justify themselves.

The big bang theory is truly no different than a flat-world theory; they are merely unsubstantiated, childish guesses that have no bearing on the actual truth, no matter how loudly they are proclaimed. How is proving that the universe is expanding, for example, proof of a big bang? And when did hypothesizing (science talk for guessing) become scientific proof? I'll answer that—never!

As it was then, so it is now; the truth of the origin of the universe is right there in the Bible. God created the heavens and the earth and everything in them. As always, the Bible, not man's wisdom will prove to be the standard of truth.

## The greatest fear of my life was turning away from the teachings of the Mormon Church.

With the truths I've learned from the Bible, I have been set free from fear and have found deliverance from my past sins. It is now my great desire that others will also come to see that you don't have to be afraid anymore. You don't have to be held hostage by your family, your feelings, or your emotions; the choice is yours. In the end, it will be God we all face—not our wives, husbands, fathers, mothers, friends, or family.

The Bible is the Word of God, and by its truths alone you will have all the tools and knowledge needed to stand before God boldly and uncondemned, rather than unworthy. That standing will come, not from any righteousness of your own, but truly through the righteousness of the only right one, Jesus Christ.

In all meekness and with a tender heart for all who may be seeking answers, I will show that the teachings of the Mormon church need only be held against the Word of God to be proven false. I find no need for half-truths and arrogant slanders against the members whose desire for godliness and zeal for the Lord are good. These are honorable people with every right to believe what they choose.

Now let's begin a study and comparison of the Mormon beliefs as stated in the Thirteen Articles of Faith versus biblical Christianity.

May the God of truth and peace bless you richly with the understanding of His Word. May you come to know what is the height, the depth and width of His love and be saved into His kingdom; in the mighty name of Jesus Christ (Yeshua of Nazareth, Immanuel).

# Chapter 2

## Truth Is Truth, Wherever You Find It

THERE ARE PRINCIPLES common among most religions of the world. For example, the biblical teaching, "whatsoever a man soweth, that shall he also reap" (Galatians 6:7), is similar to the idea of karma in the Buddhist religion. In the secular world, they say "What comes around goes around." In the Qur'an it is expressed thus: "If you do good, you do good for yourselves; and if you do evil, [you do it] to yourselves" (Qur'an 17:7).

As we look at the doctrines of the Mormon faith, it is neither my desire nor intention to refute every teaching. There are elements of truth in most religions; I wish only to address the teachings that simply do not line up with the truth of God's Word

---

## The Thirteen Articles of Faith

The Thirteen Articles of Faith came originally from a letter that Joseph Smith Jr. wrote to an associate explaining the basic tenets of the Mormon faith. It was later adopted as the official statement of faith of the church. Joseph Smith, the founding leader of the Mormon faith, was considered a major prophet of God and held in very high regard by the members of the church .

These Articles explain the beliefs every Mormon is expected to accept in order to be baptized into the church. On face value, they sound very Christian and biblically sound.

## Who is Joseph Smith Jr. in the eyes of the LDS people?

While they do not worship him, they hold him at the level of Moses and even just under Christ. Mormons believe Joseph Smith was given the task of restoring the original church set up by Christ Himself. They believe the church that Joseph established is the Lord's only true church on the earth. John Taylor, an early church leader stated in his record:

"Joseph Smith, the Prophet and Seer of the Lord, has done more, save Jesus only, for the salvation of men in this world, than any other man that ever lived in it. In the short space of twenty years, he has brought forth the Book of Mormon, which he translated by the gift and power of God, and has been the means of publishing it on two continents; has sent the fullness of the everlasting gospel, which it contained, to the four quarters of the earth; has brought forth the revelations and commandments which compose this book of Doctrine and Covenants, and many other wise documents and instructions for the benefit of the children of men; gathered many thousands of the Latter-day Saints, founded a great city, and left a fame and name that cannot be slain. He lived great, and he died great in the eyes of God and his people; and like most of the Lord's anointed in ancient times, has sealed his mission and his works with his own blood; and so has his brother Hyrum" (Doctrine and Covenants 135:3).

## We have the words "Jesus Christ" in our name—how can you say we are not Christian?

Despite the title of this book, I do not disagree with all thirteen articles of faith; however, over all the differences between what these words mean to a Mormon and what those same words mean to a traditional Christian are vast. These differences are so great that they hold our very salvation in the balance.

It is not me, but the teachings of the Bible that are in direct opposition to the real intent of the Thirteen Articles. If these words meant the same thing to a Mormon that they do as stated in the Bible, they would mostly be of great value. As they stand, however, if followed, they can never lead one to heaven, nor salvation.

In this book, I will take each key word used in the various Articles and simply show what is meant in a Mormon's understanding as stated by their own leaders and what was taught to me personally from birth to age thirty-three. You must understand that Mormon leaders are not like typical Christian leaders. They are claimed to be the "very mouthpieces of God" who's words are taught to be as new scripture to the members. Therefore, I will use their words not mine to show the vast gap between what they mean by the words chosen versus what is taught in the Bible.

## What's in a word?

When Mormons are taught words such as *salvation, Jesus Christ, God,* and many others, they do not have the same meanings as a Christian would understand them from a biblical perspective. This is why it is not enough to use the same words, if the meanings are completely different.

Mormons are constant these days in making this statement: "How can they say we are not Christians when we have the words 'Jesus Christ' in the name of our church?" I will address this great question by bringing to light a similar situation that occurs within the Islamic faith.

## What's in a name?

When Muslims use the term "Allah," we commonly assume this name is merely an Arabic word for the God of the Bible. Allah, however, is not just another name for the one we understand as God. This is a different being with different attributes and characteristics than the God of the Bible.

Before the seventh century, Mohammed pronounced Allah as the only one true God. Note that Allah, was the widely worshipped moon god throughout ancient Mesopotamia. This can easily be verified because Allah is found in Arabic inscriptions prior to Islam's foundation.

In order to appease the pagan populations in Arabia, Mohammed chose among the various gods, Allah, who was married to the sun goddess in their legends. (Wikipedia, Allah.)

Some believe this is most likely why they use the crescent moon as the symbol of Islam (even though they attempt to explain this away.)

They also reject Jesus as the Son of God, as well as any deity that the Bible ascribes to Him. This alone proves that we are not talking about the same God. For these and other reasons, we can say that Allah is not the same God of the Bible who is without beginning of days nor end of years and is clearly the, "Son of God" according to our Bible and the truth of God's Word.

In the same way, the Mormons use the names "Jesus Christ" and "God the Eternal Father" to describe two persons that actually do not exist in the form, function, or character in which they claim. (We will go over the ramifications of this statement shortly.)

The Mormons, then, are not talking about the same Being as stated in the Bible any more than Muslims are talking about the same God. Let's get started with our comparison.

# Chapter 3

## The First Article of Faith

*Article 1. We believe in God, the Eternal Father, and in His Son, Jesus Christ, and in the Holy Ghost.*

## What does a Mormon mean when he says, "We believe in God the Eternal Father"?

Mormons are taught that God is a glorified flesh-and-blood man who is now the God of all heaven and earth. He is said to look exactly like Jesus in appearance. Joseph Smith said in his own words:

I will go back to the beginning before the world was, to show what kind of being God is. What sort of a being was God in the beginning? … God himself was once as we are now, and is an exalted man, … it is necessary we should understand the character and being of God and how he came to be so; for I am going to tell you how God came to be God. We have imagined and supposed that God was God from all eternity. I will refute that idea, and take away the veil, so that you may see…. It is the first principle of the Gospel to know for a certainty the Character of God, … and that he was once a man like us; yea, that God himself, the Father of us all, dwelt on an earth, the same as Jesus Christ himself did (Smith, *Teachings of the Prophet Joseph Smith*, p. 345).

Lorenzo Snow, the fifth leader of the Mormon church also restated this concept in the words I heard throughout my whole life in primary, Sunday school, and elders quorum: "As man is, God once was. As God is, man may become."

Also, James Talmage an early member of the quorum of the LDS twelve apostles said, "Therefore we know that both the Father and the Son are in form and stature perfect men; each of them possesses a tangible body . . . of flesh and bones" (Talmage, *Articles of Faith*, p. 38).

In a *Times Magazine* interview, August 4, 1997, Gordon B. Hinckley, the fifteenth president of the LDS church, attempted to downplay this teaching. He stated in response to a question posed about the Mormon teaching that God was once a human, "That gets into some pretty deep theology that we don't know very much about."

I am a personal witness that this statement is not accurate whatsoever. I remember hearing Gordon jokingly say, in response to this very article (at a general conference I attended), "oh, we understand a lot about it."

In thirty years of faithfully going to church in many different states (my family moved a lot) and throughout my whole life to that point, there was never one question raised by the leaders as to the understanding of this doctrine. It was—and is—taught as fact to this very day.

Mormons are taught that we have a "Spirit Mother" and were birthed spiritually rather than created. Mormons are taught that God has many wives, and each of us have the same Father God, but each person, or group of persons, have a different Spirit Mother. This is much like earthly families where there may be two children from the first wife, then so many from the next. They could have the same father, but the mothers would be different. Mormons do not pray to the Spirit Mother or know her name, as she is not as important in their theology.

This concept is a common theme in their belief structure wherein they spiritualize every earthly act. They feel that procreation, childrearing and many other earthly activities will also be the norm for a heavenly existence.

## Mormons are taught to believe there are many gods that rule other galaxies and such.

The Mormons have many of their own writings, which they consider scripture, that talk about this concept; but they often use a text from the Bible to defend this theology. First Corinthians 8:5 says, "For though there be that are called gods, whether in heaven or in earth (as there be gods many, and lords many)." Paul is clearly talking about idols, not other actual gods. Thus in light of the many other references to the fact that there is only one God (as well as this very scripture), please note the lowercase *g* in the term "gods many," and lower case *l* in "lords many." This is because he is talking about false gods, and earthly lords. This may not be a fact to base your theology on, but look at what the text is saying: "though there *be* that are *called* gods" (emphasis added). In other words, there are many that are *called* gods, but they are just idols, not actually God. This scripture makes no argument that there are other real Gods.

Mormons also use Genesis 1:26 to prove their argument. This verse says, "And God said "Let us make man in our own image."

## The greatest fall of all time was a result of a created being wanting to become as God.

Another fact of note is that Lucifer's fall was a result of this very idea that a created being could one day be as God or attain to the position of Godhood. Isaiah 14:12–14 reads:

How art thou fallen from heaven, O Lucifer, son of the morning! How art thou cut down to the ground, which didst weaken the nations! For thou hast said in thine heart, I will ascend into heaven, I will exalt my throne above the stars of God: I will sit also upon the mount of the congregation, in the sides of the north: I will ascend above the heights of the clouds; I will be like the most High.

In Genesis 3:5, we read how Satan's temptation to Adam and Eve related this very same desire to be as God. He told them, "For God doth know that in the day ye eat thereof, then your eyes shall be opened, and ye shall be as gods, knowing good and evil."

## What are Mormons taught to believe about the Eternal Father?

I'm not trying to be mean, but I honestly have to admit I have no clue what a Mormon means by the term "Eternal Father" because He can't always have been "God the Eternal Father" and have ever been a man. Eternal means without beginning; everlasting. Likewise, if He were ever anything but God, He could not be called the Eternal Father. The mass of Scriptural evidence proves that God was always God, forever, without beginning or end.

## What does the Bible teach about God the Eternal Father?

The God of the Bible is much bigger, more awesome and incomprehensible than the man-god of the Mormons. Please bear with my weak attempts to explain Him. I think I'll start with 1 Timothy 3:16: "And *without controversy* great is *the mystery of god-liness*: God was manifest in the flesh, justified in the Spirit, seen of angels, preached unto the Gentiles, believed on in the world, received up into glory" (emphasis added.)

I can't tell you how wonderful it feels right now to be at a complete loss of words to describe the great, big, awesome wonder that is the God of the Bible. So, to paraphrase what Paul said to Timothy, "Look, Timmy, no one can even argue the fact that this Being we call God is a massive, incomprehensible mystery!"

If our God is small enough to wrap our mind around and comprehend, then He is too small to create the universe or save us from our sin.

## The Bible teaches us God is a Spirit.

The Bible clearly teaches that God does not have a body of flesh and blood, but is a Spirit. Consider the following passages.

**John 4:23–24:** "But the hour cometh, and now is, when the true worshippers shall worship the Father in spirit and in truth: for the Father seeketh such to worship him. God is a Spirit: and they that worship him must worship him in spirit and in truth."

**Luke 24:39:** "Behold my hands and my feet, that it is I myself: handle me, and see; for a spirit hath not flesh and bones, as ye see me have."

**1 Timothy 1:17:** "Now unto the King eternal, immortal, invisible, the only wise God, be honour and glory for ever and ever. Amen."

**Numbers 23:19:** "God is not a man that he should lie; neither the son of man, that he should repent: hath he said, and shall he not do it? or hath he spoken, and shall he not make it good?"

Here is the truth of the Bible on the nature of God. God is not, nor has He ever been, a man with a separate body from Jesus. God is not, nor has He ever been a man with a body on another earth as a begotten Son to another God as Jesus was "the Son of man."

I am fully aware the Mormons have their writings that would change this fact; they would have to. You can trust the Word of God, the Bible. God is a Spirit—you need not fear their teaching of anything otherwise.

## The Bible teaches us God is eternal.

It is impossible for the God of the Bible to have had a beginning.

**Psalm 41:13:** Blessed be the LORD God of Israel from everlasting, and to everlasting. Amen, and Amen.

**Psalm 90:2:** Before the mountains were brought forth, or ever thou hadst formed the earth and the world, even from everlasting to everlasting, thou art God.

**1 Timothy 1:17:** Now unto the King eternal, immortal, invisible, the only wise God, be honour and glory for ever and ever. Amen.

**Malachi 3:6:** For I am the LORD, I change not; therefore ye sons of Jacob are not consumed.

**Revelation 1:8:** I am Alpha and Omega, the beginning and the ending, saith the Lord, which is, and which was, and which is to come, the Almighty.

## What is God like?

The eternal nature of God has always been expressed in a threefold form. This is why in Genesis the Bible reads, "Let us make man in our own image." According to the Bible, there has always been an aspect of God's character that fills all things and is known as the Father. There has always been an aspect of God's character that is physical, both seen and unseen, known as the Word. Through the Word all things were created, all powers in heaven and earth set forth, and all things are held in their created form. The Word is Jesus Christ. There has also always been an aspect of the character of God that moves the created and testifies to the created the truth of God by which all truth is taught and understood. This is the Holy Spirit, who also is the power of God.

God is eternal; He has no beginning and no end. Revelation 1:8 says, "I am Alpha and Omega, the beginning and the ending, saith the Lord, which is, and which was, and which is to come, the Almighty." In Revelation 4:8, those around the heavenly throne affirm: "Holy, holy, holy, LORD God Almighty, which was, and is, and is to come." Thus our God is, always and forever, God the Eternal Father.

## The Bible teaches us there is only one God.

The term *Elohim*, translated "the Gods," is what throws many off. This is where Christianity begins to separate from Mormonism in earnest. God has always existed in three functions, or parts, if you will.

God's character is not made as the Mormons teach: $1+1+1=3$, or three separate beings acting as one, all of whom have already attained to the "office" of God; as in lords many and gods many. The equation of the biblical God looks rather like: $1 \times 1 \times 1 = 1$, one God with three parts. There are many examples of triunity in nature as well. One of the most compelling is the atom. Atoms are made of three parts: proton, neutron, and electron. While each part has a distinct job, they make up only one atom. $1 \times 1 \times 1 = 1$ atom. This may be construed as mere logic though, so let's hear from the Word of God to propel the thought:

**1 Corinthians 8:4–6:** As concerning therefore the eating of those things that are offered in sacrifice unto idols, we know that an idol is nothing in the world, and that there is none other God but one. For though there be that are called gods, whether in heaven or in earth (as there be gods many, and lords many), but to us there is but one God, the Father, of whom are all things, and we in him; and one Lord Jesus Christ, by whom are all things, and we by him.

**Galatians 3:20:** Now a mediator is not a mediator of one, but God is one.

**1 Timothy 2:5:** For there is one God, and one mediator between God and men, the man Christ Jesus.

**Isaiah 45:18:** For thus saith the LORD that created the heavens; God himself that formed the earth and made it;… I am the LORD; and there is none else.

**James 2:19:** Thou believest that there is one God; thou doest well; the devils also believe, and tremble.

Many other scriptures teach this as well. There is overwhelming scriptural evidence that there is only one God now, and there has always been only one God for all time and eternity. Do not be in fear over the scriptures they present that downplay this fact or change it or add to it or take away. Stand on the Word of God and know that there is only one God—even if you can't, as I said, wrap your mind around the concept.

Any other God with any other makeup is not the God of the Bible and has no more power to save than an inanimate, lifeless idol. Genesis 1:1 says, "In the beginning, God [Elohim] [Father, Son, and Holy Ghost] created the heavens and earth." He did this through the will of the Father, the power of the Spirit, and the command of the spoken Word (the Son of God who always says what He hears the Father saying). "Let there be" He said, "and it was so."

# Chapter 4

*Article 1. We believe in God, the Eternal Father, and in His Son, Jesus Christ, and in the Holy Ghost.*

**...and in His Son, Jesus Christ...**

(*continuation of the first article of faith*)

$\mathcal{C}$ONTINUING ON WITH the first Article of Faith, let's discuss the Mormon concept of Jesus. This is the most important chapter of this book; I pray the Father will touch you with this vital truth I am about to share.

## What the Mormons mean when they say "and in His Son, Jesus Christ"

Please note that the following doctrines, are from Mormon prophets or leaders, not anti-Mormon authors.

## Mormons are taught to believe Jesus was the first spirit to be born in heaven rather than an eternal part of the triune nature of God.

Apostle McConkie wrote, "The first spirit to be born in heaven was Jesus" (*Mormon Doctrine*, p. 129). Joseph F. Smith, sixth prophet of the LDS church said, "Among the spirit children of Elohim, the firstborn was and is Jehovah, or Jesus Christ, to whom all others are juniors" (*Gospel Doctrine*, p. 70).

## Mormons are taught to believe Jesus and Satan are spirit brothers, and we were all born as siblings in heaven (*Mormon Doctrine*, p. 163; *Gospel Through the Ages*, p. 15).

The Mormons believe that Jesus and Lucifer were both spirit brothers. This means that Jesus was also merely a spirit child of the Father just like Satan was before he fell.

## Mormons are taught that the spirit of man is not a created being

Mormon teaching states that: "The spirit of man is not a created being; it existed from eternity." History of the church, page 387 Deseret news 1905)

This is why it is conceivable to them that God could have once been a mortal man because He, too, would of course be "eternal."

According to the Bible, however, man is not eternal but, like the angels, is a created being. Man's spirit came into existence when God breathed into his nostrils "the breath of life" (his spirit). At that point, man became a living soul. "And the LORD God formed man of the dust of the ground, and breathed into his nostrils the breath of life; and man became a living soul" (Genesis 3:7).

He became a living soul the moment God breathed life into him; before this, man was just a lump of lifeless clay. No matter how logical it may sound to have been in a pre-earth existence, if it's not the truth of God's Word, it's false. God's foreknowledge is not a basis for the preexistence of mankind.

God created us first naturally, then, as He breaths the breath of life into us, we are created spiritually into a living soul. We were never in exlstence in heaven before we were born, as we didn't yet exist. Consider the words of 1 Corinthians 15:45–46: "And so it is written, The first man Adam was made a living soul; the last Adam was made a quickening spirit. Howbeit that was not first which is spiritual, but that which is natural; and afterward that which is spiritual." This clearly shows that the natural was created before the spiritual. This in direct opposition to the Mormon preexistence doctrine.

Scriptures such as Jeremiah 1:5 are examples of God's foreknowledge, not evidence of preexistence: "Before I formed thee in the belly I knew thee; and before thou camest forth out of the womb I sanctified thee, and I ordained thee a prophet unto the nations." This is a wonderful picture that shows that each one of us is created on purpose. We have a destiny in Christ, and we are known by our loving Father in Heaven.

Before we are formed in the womb, our Father knows the beginning to the end of our lives. All things past and present are before Him. The Bible tells us that God's plans for our lives are for good (Jeremiah 29:11). We must, however, choose to step into that destiny of our own free will.

## Mormons are taught God chose Jesus over Lucifer to save mankind.

According to their teachings, there was a "preexistence counsel" in heaven, wherein God asked who He would send to make atonement for the coming sins of mankind that would be inevitable. Jesus stood and said, "here am I, send me and the glory be thine forever" (Moses 4:2 D&C of the Church of the LDS Church).

Lucifer stood and offered his services but claimed he would lose none (to hell). He would do this by taking away our free-will/agency, the catch was that he wanted the glory for himself (Moses 4:1 D&C of the Church of the LDS Church). Lucifer's plan was rejected, a war ensued and Lucifer was cast out with his followers to earth.

While they do not believe in the eternal deity of Jesus as part of the triune nature of God, they do call their Jesus "Savior" and "Lord" because they believe He paid for the sins of those who accept the LDS teachings, both alive and those who except it after they die through "vicarious baptism for the dead" and other vicarious ordinances that are performed on behalf of the dead by their family.

It is taught by the Mormons that Jesus's death on the cross made it possible for everyone to be resurrected, both believers and nonbelievers—which is true. Yet, they reject the biblical teaching that salvation is apart from works. They teach instead that, at a minimum, the following things must take place before you can be with God, Jesus, and the Holy Ghost:

1. One must be baptized into the LDS church and remain worthy/faithful until death (or if one didn't hear their gospel while alive, come to the Lord and receive the ordinances done by a living person on their behalf after death through temple work).

2. Receive the Holy Ghost by the "laying on of the hands" by recognized leaders.

3. Receive the priesthood if male, and if female, get married in an LDS temple to a Mormon male who has the priesthood. They call this being "sealed [together] for time and all eternity." They must do this temple service in order to receive their "endowments," which qualifies them to be exalted if they are found worthy at the judgment.

Being "exalted" is what Christians refer to as being "saved." Exalted persons will be the only ones who will live forever with all three of the Godhead, consisting of God the Father, Jesus Christ, and the Holy Ghost. Sadly, according to the teachings of Joseph Smith, even after doing all this, they have no assurance of salvation (exaltation) until after they die and are judged.

Mormons are taught they will then be able to have spirit children of their own and advance to the "office of Godhood." The men will have many wives and innumerable spirit children. These new heavenly families will be together forever as a separate family unit after death and upon receiving exaltation.

**Bruce R. McConkie taught that Jesus's birth was the result of a natural sex act between God the Father and Mary, rather than a supernatural move of the Holy Spirit.**

Bruce R. McConkie, a member of the church's quorum of the twelve apostles, stated "Christ was begotten by an Immortal Father in the same way that mortal men are begotten by mortal fathers" (*Mormon Doctrine*, by Bruce McConkie, p. 547). "The birth of the Saviour was as natural as are the births of our children; it was the result of natural action. He partook of flesh and blood—was begotten of his Father, as we were of our fathers" (*Journal of Discourses*, vol. 8, p. 115). "He was not born without the aid of Man, and that Man was God." (*Doctrines of Salvation*, by Joseph Fielding Smith, 1954, 1:18).

**Mormons are taught that Jesus paid for our sins in the garden of Gethsemane more so than on the cross.**

Apostle Bruce McConkie stated "Where and under what circumstances was the atoning sacrifice of the Son of God made? Was it on the Cross of Calvary or in the Garden of Gethsemane? It is to the Cross of Christ that most Christians look when centering their attention upon the infinite and eternal atonement. And certainly the sacrifice of our Lord was completed when he was lifted up by men; also, that part of his life and suffering is more dramatic and, perhaps, more soul stirring. But in reality the pain and suffering, the triumph and grandeur, of the atonement took place primarily in Gethsemane" [where he bled from every pour] (*Doctrinal New Testament Commentary*, vol. 1, p. 774).

**Mormon leaders such as Brigham Young taught that not all sins were paid for at the cross, but some such as murder and repeated adultery must be atoned for by the blood of the individual.**

Brigham Young and other leaders whom Mormons believe to be the mouthpieces of God taught; "Jesus' sacrifice was not able to cleanse us from sins such as murder and repeated adultery."

They taught instead that a man's own blood must atone for these types of sins. Brigham Young stated the following: "If you find your brother in bed with your wife, and you put a javelin through them both, you would be justified and they would [have] atoned for their sins and be received into the kingdom of God. ... There is not a man or woman, who violates the covenants made with their God, that will not be required to pay the debt. The blood of Christ will never wipe that out, your own blood must atone for it" (*Journal of Discourses,* vol. 3, p. 247).

Let's be real—when you attribute the kind of direct-revelation-from-God authority to the leadership that the LDS church attributes to its leaders, it matters little whether or not this is an official teaching of the church. It was a discourse or sermon taught by a founding leader of the church. If the mouthpiece of God—a Mormon prophet—could be this wrong about a basic idea of salvation, it should make the wise then look to many other things he taught and begin to question the validity of those as well.

## What does the Bible teach about Jesus?

Please understand, friend, the most important beliefs in religion are what a person believes about Jesus Christ, and what he/she does about that belief.

## Jesus is the only way.

Christ Himself taught in John 14:6: "I am the way, the truth, and the life: no man cometh unto the Father, but by me." Jesus is the only way to get to God, to life eternal, and to the kingdom of heaven to come, according to the Bible. Therefore, if you miss the mark on this one concept, there is no hope of salvation. Jesus said again in John 10:7–10:

"Verily, verily, I say unto you, I am the door of the sheep. All that ever came before me are thieves and robbers: but the sheep did not hear them. I am the door: by me if any man enter in, he shall be saved, and shall go in and out, and find pasture. The thief cometh not, but for to steal, and to kill, and to destroy: I am come that they might have life, and that they might have it more abundantly."

Jesus is the door. If you come to God by any other way, any other name, you are not one of His.

Jesus said again in Matthew 24:24: "For there shall arise false Christs, and false prophets, and shall shew great signs and wonders; insomuch that, if it were possible, they shall deceive the very elect."

A "Christ" who does not have the attributes, character, or deity of the true Jesus of Nazareth, as taught in the Bible, is a false Christ and has no power to bring you to the Father. He is instead a robber and a thief; a cursing, not a savior.

## Jesus was either what He claimed to be or a raving lunatic.

I have met many people on the streets of the inner city where I minister. I often ask those I meet, who Jesus is to them. Many say things like Jesus was a good person; Jesus was a prophet; or Jesus was a great teacher. However, it is abundantly clear from the Bible that Jesus claimed to be equal with God. He was, therefore, either what he claimed to be, or a raving lunatic. Let me explain: if someone went around today saying he was the actual Son of God, he would be put in a home. No one would think, "Wow, this crazy guy is a real good teacher." Even if he did some really wonderful things, if he thinks he is the actual Son of God (which would make him a God, too) and he's not, then he is a liar and a deceiver, not a good person, nor a great teacher etc. Jesus said of himself, "I came out from God" (John 16:27), as well as "I came out from thee" (John 17:8), and again "I and my Father are one" (John 10:30).

If these things are not true—if He is anything less than who He said he was—then he is not a "good person." A good person wouldn't make such weighty comments if they weren't true. I can hear it now—"Well, ya know, little JC's a pretty good kid, he does well on his homework, helps around the house... So we overlook the fact that he thinks he's the Son of God. We just think it's so cute!" Ridiculous, right? Praise be to God, however, Jesus is exactly who He said He was.

## What is the real Jesus like then?

The most important aspect of the true Messiah was that His coming must fulfill every "jot and tittle" (Old English for every punctuation mark) of the law. He must come in the way prophesied and He must have the attributes, the power, and must perform the miracles that were predicted. The Jews didn't miss Christ because He didn't fulfill these requirements; they missed Him because He didn't come in the way they wanted Him to.

The Jewish people were filled with self-righteousness and pride and weren't looking for spiritual healing; they wanted a political savior. After all, they were the chosen people of God through Abraham. They were in the "only true church on earth." However, Christ soon revealed to them that just being in the chosen lineage (the right church) was not the only answer. Romans 2:28–29 says, "For he is not a Jew, which is one outwardly; neither is that circumcision, which is outward in the flesh: But he is a Jew, which is one inwardly; and circumcision is that of the heart, in the spirit, and not in the letter; whose praise is not of men, but of God."

It was a matter of whether or not they accepted the promised Savior. They must accept the Messiah and His message of love and grace and receive His sacrifice for their sin from the heart. Not just another list of do's and don'ts, not just by association.

## The Bible teaches that Jesus is the only way to God.

As it is written in 1 John 5:12, "He that hath the Son hath life; and he that hath not the Son of God hath not life." In order to "have" the Son, you must know Him. To know Him, you must know His word. Jesus said in John 5:39, "Search the scriptures; for in them ye think ye have eternal life: and they are they which testify of me."

The Bible clearly set forth for us what the Messiah would be like and who He was. Let's look at a few key aspects of the Jesus Christ of the Bible.

## The Bible teaches us Jesus is Immanuel, God with us.

Isaiah 7:14 says: "Therefore the Lord himself shall give you a sign; Behold, a virgin shall conceive, and bear a son, and shall call his name Immanuel." Among other things, the Messiah must be born of a virgin, the Messiah must be "God with us," not only our "older [spirit] brother." He is not just a begotten son of a virgin; He is not just a glorified man with God's Spirit in Him. Immanuel means *God with us.* He is God, come to dwell with us. This was clarified in the New Testament in Matthew 1:23: "Behold, a virgin shall be with child, and shall bring forth a son, and they shall call his name Emmanuel, which being interpreted is, God with us."

The Word of God says that in the mouth of two or three witnesses, every word would be established, so here's more. "For unto us a child is born, unto us a son is given: and the government shall be upon his shoulder: and his name shall be called Wonderful, Counselor, The mighty God, The everlasting Father, The Prince of Peace" (Isaiah 9:6).

There are some very key points here to look at. First, the child born unto us was Jesus, no Christian disputes this. Second, this son will be "the mighty God, the everlasting Father, the Prince of Peace. A prince is a *son* of a king. This would make the Messiah to come both Father and Son. This concept from a human standpoint is just plain foolishness and the stumbling block for most people who do not except the Christ of the Bible. However, with God "all things are possible." Let me explain it the best I can. As always, let's start with what the Word of God has to say about it.

"In the beginning was the Word, and the Word was with God, and the Word was God. The same was in the beginning with God. All things were made by him; and without him was not anything made that was made. In him was life; and the life was the light of men. And the light shineth in darkness; and the darkness comprehended it not." (John 1:1–5)

Before Messiah came to earth, He was in the beginning with God as the "Word." He is the Jehovah of the Old Testament, and He is the spoken Word of God by which all things come into existence. Jesus made this very claim when he said in John 8:58, "Before Abraham was, I am."

Jesus was doing more here than just saying He was around before Abraham. He was using the same name for Himself He gave to Moses at the burning bush: "And God said unto Moses, I AM THAT I AM: and he said, Thus shalt thou say unto the children of Israel, I AM hath sent me unto you" (Exodus 3:14).

Jesus also said in John 6:62, "What and if ye shall see the Son of man ascend up where he was before?" We know it was not the Father that Moses or Abraham saw, because according to John 1:18, no human has at any time seen God. "No man hath seen God at any time; the only begotten Son, which is in the bosom of the Father, he hath declared him."

From the very beginning, Jesus has been the declaration of the glory of the Father. So when Abraham, Moses, and others "saw the Lord," it could not have been the Father but a revelation, or declaration of the Father, given through Jesus—Immanuel.

When Jesus was born of the Holy Spirit, the aspect of God that is the Word came into the world as a son. He was called the Son of man because He took on flesh. Thus, the Son of man was altogether a man, and altogether God; because the part of the Godhead that was with God from the beginning, the Word, came into flesh and dwelt among us. When you look at Jesus, you are actually looking at God in the form of a man.

Consider John 14:9: "Jesus saith unto him, Have I been so long time with you, and yet hast thou not known me, Philip? He that hath seen me hath seen the Father; and how sayest thou then, Shew us the Father?" Jesus was not saying this because He and God are like twins; no, He said what he meant—if you have seen Jesus, you have seen the Father. In order to explain this further, let's look at Colossians 1:13–19.

"Who hath delivered us from the power of darkness, and hath translated us into the kingdom of his dear Son: In whom we have redemption through his blood, even the forgiveness of sins: Who is the image of the invisible God, the firstborn of every creature: For by him were all things created, that are in heaven, and that are in earth, visible and invisible, whether they be thrones, or dominions, or principalities, or powers: all things were created by him, and for him: And he is before all things, and by him all things consist. And he is the head of the body, the church: who is the beginning, the firstborn from the dead; that in all things he might have the preeminence. For it pleased the Father that in him should all fulness [of the Godhead] dwell."

God is an invisible Spirit. Jesus is the tangible manifestation of God into the world. In order to honor the Son, God placed all of the fullness of the Godhead within Jesus. Colossians 2:9 reiterates this: "For in him dwelleth all the fulness of the Godhead bodily." This is why we worship the Lord Jesus Christ, because He is God with us. He is both the Prince of Peace and the Everlasting Father. God has not ceased to be God but has, Himself, decided to honor the Son in this way. This is why when we pray, we pray to the Father "in the name of Jesus."

There are many other things I can say about Jesus, but this is the point: Jesus is Immanuel—God with us. If you do not know this Jesus, then you are not able to come to the Father. No other Jesus, with other origins, other attributes, or one who is not an eternal member of the Godhead, is the promised Messiah.

Please understand that my heart is tender when I must be very blunt here. If the only way to the Father is by coming to the Son, you had better really know who He is. If you believe in a different being than the one described in the Bible, you are coming up some other way. Every false religion of the world has this same error. They miss the mark on who the Son of God is, and that keeps their followers captive. Not that they do this knowingly—they are themselves deceived and blind to the truth. This is not a statement against the people. I have met many wonderful Muslims, Mormons, and Jehovah's Witnesses. All these and others like them have a key flaw in theology, wherein they change the character of Christ and therefore are not able to come to God through their teachings. I love all people; the organizations and their teachings are what I must protest; not the wonderful people.

Because of this deception regarding who the Son of God is, the Mormon faith does not lead to salvation. Its teachings do not lead one to Christianity because they present a false Christ. Without intervention from God, no one in the Mormon faith would be saved, based strictly on the teachings presented. Praise God, however, because He wants to be found and will be found by all true seekers. God is not running and hiding from you, friend. It is His desire that none should be lost. God has made us who we are for a purpose. I was raised a Mormon with no fault or knowledge of my own. Many are born into other non-redemptive religions in the same way. Once I heard the truth, however, it was then up to me to decide what to do about it. I had to make a choice. Should I keep my family happy, or should I follow the Word of God? For me, the choice was very difficult but never a question. I chose the Lord. The Lord used everything I learned to help me. He truly worked all things together for my good—just as He will for anyone who chooses to follow the Word of the Lord, even at the loss of all earthly things.

Everything that I lost due to my decision to follow the Word of God and not the Mormon faith has been more than compensated by the peace that I now enjoy. I lost many things. I have suffered for my choice; but I would rather suffer now than be lost forever.

## What does the Bible teach about pre-earth existence and spirits?

There are at least four types of spirits mentioned in the Bible: the Spirit of God, ministering spirits to God, ministering spirits for man, and the fallen, evil spirits banished from heaven for rebelling against God.

Let's look at some supportive verses for each of these spirit types. First, the ultimate Spirit, the Spirit of God: "God is a Spirit, and they that worship Him must worship Him in Spirit and in Truth" (John 4:24).

Second, there are spirits/beings created to minister to God constantly through worship. Revelation 1:4 tells of the "seven Spirits which are before his throne." Revelation 4:8 says there are four beasts, each of which has "six wings about him; and they were full of eyes within: and they rest not day and night, saying, Holy, holy, holy, LORD God Almighty, which was, and is, and is to come."

Third, there are ministering angels created to minister to God on behalf and for the heirs of salvation. Hebrews 1:14 declares, "Are they not all ministering spirits, sent forth to minister for them who shall be heirs of salvation?" Psalm 104:4 and Hebrews 1:7 both say that God "maketh his angels spirits, and his ministers a flaming fire."

Finally, there are those spirits who fell from the presence of God, who are now known as evil spirits. Revelation 12:4 tells about the dragon. "And his tail drew the third part of the stars of heaven, and did cast them to the earth: and the dragon stood before the woman which was ready to be delivered, for to devour her child as soon as it was born."

Of all created spirits, it is apparent that Lucifer was the nearest to the throne or mercy seat of God. Lucifer's job was to shield the glory of God as a cherub that covers the ark of the covenant. Exodus 25:22 says, "And there I will meet with thee, and I will commune with thee from above the mercy seat, from between the two cherubims which are upon the ark of the testimony, of all things which I will give thee in commandment unto the children of Israel." 1 Kings 8:7 continues the description: "For the cherubims spread forth their two wings over the place of the ark, and the cherubims covered the ark and the staves thereof above."

It is also likely that Lucifer was a lead worshiper. Ezekiel 28:13 describes him this way: "Thou hast been in Eden the garden of God; every precious stone was thy covering, the sardius, topaz, and the diamond, the beryl, the onyx, and the jasper, the sapphire, the emerald, and the carbuncle, and gold: the workmanship of thy tabrets [a percussion instrument used to praise] and of thy pipes [most likely to sing or play worship] was prepared in thee in the day that thou wast created."

There is just too much information in the next scripture references to leave any out, so I've included Ezekiel 28:14–17 and Isaiah 14:12–16 here.

**Ezekiel 28:14–17:** "Thou art the anointed cherub that covereth; and I have set thee so: thou wast upon the holy mountain of God; thou hast walked up and down in the midst of the stones of fire. *[See Psalm 104:4.]* Thou wast perfect in thy ways from the day that thou wast created *[note: Lucifer was a created being, not eternal as claimed by the Mormons]*, till iniquity was found in thee. By the multitude of thy merchandise they have filled the midst of thee with violence, and thou hast sinned: therefore I will cast thee as profane out of the mountain of God: and I will destroy thee, O covering cherub, from the midst of the stones of fire. Thine heart was lifted up because of thy beauty, thou hast corrupted thy wisdom by reason of thy brightness: I will cast thee to the ground, I will lay thee before kings, that they may behold thee."

**Isaiah 14:12–16:** "How art thou fallen from heaven, O Lucifer, son of the morning! how art thou cut down to the ground, which didst weaken the nations! For thou hast said in thine heart, I will ascend into heaven, I will exalt my throne above the stars of God: I will sit also upon the mount of the congregation, in the sides of the north: I will ascend above the heights of the clouds; I will be like the most High. Yet thou shalt be brought down to hell, to the sides of the pit. They that see thee shall narrowly look upon thee, and consider thee, saying, Is this the man that made the earth to tremble, that did shake kingdoms?"

The word of God is very clear: Lucifer was a created being of perfect beauty. This beauty caused him to be filled with pride. He wanted to exalt himself and be "like the most High." Lucifer was not Jesus's brother. He was a ministering spirit that got too *bright* for his own good; he is a created being.

Jesus, on the other hand, was with God from the beginning. He is not a created being and stands far above as Lord of all. Only the Son of man (His flesh) was made a little lower than the angels because He had to suffer death. "But we see Jesus, who was made a little lower than the angels for the suffering of death, crowned with glory and honour; that he by the grace of God should taste death for every man" (Hebrews 2:9).

The mere act of putting Jesus on the same level as all of us by calling Him simply an older brother—and most assuredly a brother of Lucifer—denies His deity more than any other teaching the Mormons put out. Jesus is called our "older brother" only because He was the first born from the dead.

**The Bible teaches that Christ was born of a virgin—one who never had sexual relations until after the birth—by the power of the Holy Ghost, not of flesh.**

It is important to note that even Mormons say the Holy Ghost has no body of flesh and blood. There is no dispute between Mormons and Christians over the fact that Mary was a virgin.

The difference would be that Christians believe she was a virgin until after she delivered Jesus. (Many Mormons also believe this, despite the teaching of their leaders.)

Simple reason alone would tell us that if God had sexual relations with Mary, she would no longer have been a virgin. Therefore, it would no longer have been a "virgin birth." Many virgins have gotten pregnant after having sexual relations. There is no significance of a virgin birth if Mary was only a virgin up until conception. The promised Messiah was to be born of a woman who had never had sexual relations with a man.

**Isaiah 7:14:** Therefore the Lord himself shall give you a sign; Behold, a virgin shall conceive, and bear a son, and shall call his name Immanuel.

**Luke 1:34:** Then said Mary unto the angel, How shall this be, seeing I know not a man?

**Matthew 1:25:** And [Joseph] knew her not till she had brought forth her firstborn son: and he called his name JESUS.

Mary was a virgin before the conception and Mary was a virgin until she brought forth her firstborn son. The Holy Ghost "overshadowed" Mary; He did not "know" her. It was a conception without sexual contact—a holy conception. There was no physical sex act of the Father with Mary.

**Luke 1:35:** And the angel answered and said unto her, The Holy Ghost shall come upon thee, and the power of the Highest shall overshadow thee: therefore also that holy thing which shall be born of thee shall be called the Son of God.

**Matthew 1:18:** Now the birth of Jesus Christ was on this wise: When as his mother Mary was espoused to Joseph, before they came together, she was found with child of the Holy Ghost.

## The Engagement of Mary and Joseph.

In Jewish custom, to be betrothed (engaged) was as binding as marriage. This is why Joseph considered having to "put her away" (divorce her) if she had had sex with another man, even though they were not yet officially married. Deuteronomy 22:23–24 tells us how serious a crime it was to have sex with a woman who was betrothed:

"If a damsel that is a virgin be betrothed unto an husband, and a man find her in the city, and lie with her; Then ye shall bring them both out unto the gate of that city, and ye shall stone them with stones that they die; the damsel, because she cried not, being in the city; and the man, because he hath humbled his neighbor's wife: so thou shalt put away evil from among you."

To say that Jesus was conceived any other way is to accuse God of sin. Notice that the betrothed woman is already considered a wife. Such an act would be on the same ground as adultery. To say God had relations with Mary is to say God committed an unholy act of breaking a betrothal vow. In order for this to not be an unholy act of sin, it would have to be a supernatural conception.

The Bible clearly teaches us Jesus was born of a virgin, and the father would be the Holy Ghost/God. Any Jesus born under any other circumstances is a false Christ and is not to be feared any more than a lifeless idol.

## The Bible teaches that it was only at the cross that Jesus paid for our sins.

The garden of Gethsemane was a place where Christ suffered the pain of spirit over His coming death on the cross. Christ knew what was ahead of Him. He knew the pain that would soon be His; the betrayal of his closest friends and followers. So much so that he begged God to "let this cup pass," unless there was no other way. There is no scriptural evidence for the claim that this had any part in our atonement. In fact, it is plainly set forth in scripture that only death can atone for the sin of mankind.

It wasn't Christ's pain and suffering that redeemed us, but the death at the cross followed by His resurrection from the dead.

John 3:14 says, "And as Moses lifted up the serpent in the wilderness, even so must the Son of man be lifted up." The whole meaning of the atonement was for Christ to become sin for us— for Him to be lifted up as the serpent in the Old Testament (see Numbers 21:9), so that whosoever looks toward Him would be saved. The cross alone is where Christ became a curse for us.

**Galatians 3:13:** Christ hath redeemed us from the curse of the law, being made a curse for us: for it is written, Cursed is every one that hangeth on a tree.

**Hebrews 9:15:** And for this cause he is the mediator of the new testament, that by means of death, for the redemption of the transgressions that were under the first testament, they which are called might receive the promise of eternal inheritance.

**Hebrews 9: 16–17:** For where a testament is, there must also of necessity be the death of the testator. For a testament is of force after men are dead: otherwise it is of no strength at all while the testator liveth.

Therefore, without the tree—i.e. the cross, Christ's death— there is no redemption.

## The Bible teaches Jesus paid for all of our sins.

The atonement was complete and perfect. The Bible in 1 John 1:9 teaches that the blood of Christ cleanses us from all unrighteousness. "If we confess our sins, he is faithful and just to forgive us our sins, and to cleanse us from all unrighteousness." James 2:10–11 teaches that any breaking of the Law makes you guilty of breaking the whole Law: "For whosoever shall keep the whole law, and yet offend in one point, he is guilty of all. For he that said, Do not commit adultery, said also, Do not kill. Now if thou commit no adultery, yet if thou kill, thou art become a transgressor of the law."

According to scripture then, if we say that any certain sin cannot be atoned, we are saying that none of them can be atoned. The question itself is flawed from the start. The question wouldn't be, can the blood of Jesus Christ atone for murder or repeated adultery; it would have to be, can it redeem us at all? This is due to the fact that if one is guilty of any point of the Law—even not honoring your parents—he/she is guilty of all and, therefore, worthy of death, "For the wages of sin is death" (Romans 6:23).

All unrepented sin equals death, not just what we consider the worst ones. This is why the Bible says in Romans 3:23, "For all have sinned and fall short of the glory of God." This is also why it teaches in Romans 3:10 that "none are righteous, no not one."

None of us are righteous—not even the best of us. Thus, if the blood of Christ cannot cover "all unrighteousness," we are all doomed.

## The "plan of salvation" is completely laid out in the Bible alone.

We are given the full plan of redemption in the Bible. Christ's redemption cleanses us of every sin, no matter how many or how unspeakable they may be. You can repent of your sins (repent means to change your mind for the better) and be forgiven right now. From this day forward, you can begin a process of a renewed life in Christ.

If you would like to know that all of your sins are forgiven and want to have the assurance now and forever that you are redeemed, ransomed, forgiven, and saved from hell, then turn now to the fifteenth chapter of this book. Pray with all your heart the prayer given under the heading of "Confession of Faith." You can begin the process of a renewed life of joy and peace of mind found only in Christ.

# Chapter 5

*Article 1. We believe in God, the Eternal Father, and in His Son, Jesus Christ, and in the Holy Ghost.*

**...and in the Holy Ghost...**

**(*continuation of the first article of faith*)**

ᏚONTINUING IN OUR discussion of the first Article of Faith, let's move on to the Mormon concept of the Holy Ghost.

## Mormons are taught that the Holy Ghost is a separate "personage" from God and not part of the same triune nature of God (D&C 130:22).

This issue falls back to the question of the nature of God in general and needs little clarification. (See "What the Bible teaches about the nature of God," chapter two.) The Mormons are taught that the Holy Ghost is a separate person from God—a person without a body who has the task of teaching, comforting, and enlightening the mind to the truthfulness of the gospel of Jesus Christ. There are many functions of the Holy Ghost to which we do not disagree. It is, as I have stated, only the nature of who He really is and how He falls within the triune nature of God that is different, yet very important. This is another point to which the Mormon church is leading its members to a false God that does not exist.

**Mormons are taught to place all of their faith (as to the truthfulness of the Mormon doctrine) on a feeling called the "burning of the bosom."**

"And when ye shall receive these things, I would exhort you that ye would ask God, the Eternal Father, in the name of Christ, if these things are not true; and if ye shall ask with a sincere heart, with real intent, having faith in Christ, he will manifest the truth of it unto you, by the power of the Holy Ghost." **Moroni 10:4:** (Book of Mormon)

It is also stated in the Doctrine and Covenants of the LDS Church (D&C 9:8) "But, behold, I say unto you, that you must study it out in your mind; then you must ask me if it be right, and if it is right I will cause that your bosom shall burn within you; therefore, you shall feel that it is right."

## What does the Bible teach about the Holy Ghost (the Holy Spirit)?

The Bible teaches us that the Holy Spirit is a permanent coeternal part of the triune nature of God. The word *triune* is not in the Bible. The word is an attempt by mortal man to describe an indescribable, immortal God. To return to the analogy of the atom, we can see the evidence of how something can be three parts yet one. We are still at a loss to understand how the three ever started being one. If you break up or split this bond, the whole thing blows up. It is the same with God. The Holy Spirit is an inseparable part of the nature of God.

Just as the Word is both "with God" and "is God," the Holy Ghost goes out from God and is God. He is the part of God's nature that comforts, fills the heart of every believer, teaches, leads, guides, empowers, changes us, renews us, emboldens us, speaks through us, and more.

We can go back to the conception of Jesus to see that the Spirit of God is also God. Matthew 1:18 says, "Now the birth of Jesus Christ was on this wise: When as his mother Mary was espoused to Joseph, before they came together, she was found with child of the Holy Ghost." We see here that Mary got pregnant by the Holy Ghost. Yet it is common scriptural knowledge that God is Jesus's Father. Luke 3:22 tells us that "a voice [came] from heaven saying, "Thou art my beloved Son; in thee I am well pleased."

This is because the Holy Spirit is from God and is God.

## When the Bible talks about blasphemy against the Holy Ghost, it is not talking about the Mormon concept of the Holy Ghost.

It is recorded in the Bible that to deny the Holy Ghost is an unforgivable sin: "And whosoever shall speak a word against the Son of man, it shall be forgiven him: but unto him that blasphemeth against the Holy Ghost it shall not be forgiven" (Luke 12:10).

Do not fear this scripture in reference to Mormon teachings as they would have you to. This is one of many fear tactics the church uses to keep people in bondage. Of course, they don't think of it this way. Mormons are wonderful, well-meaning people; they wouldn't knowingly deceive people. It is the truth, nonetheless. They are deceived because they don't understand the Word of God.

You are not speaking blasphemy against the Holy Ghost by calling a false god what he is, a false prophet what he is and a false spirit what he is. If a spirit or angel (or a feeling) or any other thing teaches you another gospel than the one in the Bible, it is a curse of the devil. Galatians 1:8 says, "But though we, or an angel from heaven, preach any other gospel unto you than that which we have preached unto you, let him be accursed."

Search the Word of God—the Bible—and you will know the truth, and the truth shall deliver you from their false teachings.

## The Workings of the Holy Spirit.

Even before the Holy Spirit was given as a "gift" at Pentecost, He has always had the duty of enlightening the hearts of holy men and women of God. Once the Son of God was manifested in the world and then glorified, the true believers of Christ could then have the Holy Spirit as a constant companion and indwelling presence. Before this time, there were only periodic manifestations, as was common in the days of the prophets.

When Christ was on the earth, the Holy Spirit was not yet an indwelling presence because Immanuel (God Himself in Christ) was present. "But this spake he of the Spirit, which they that believe on him should receive: for the Holy Ghost was not yet given; because that Jesus was not yet glorified" (John 7:39).

While they had the Word of God—Jesus—with them, they could ask Him, and He would openly teach them, "the mysteries of the kingdom…"

"He answered and said unto them, Because it is given unto you to know the mysteries of the kingdom of heaven, but to them it is not given" (Matthew 13:11).

He sent the Holy Spirit, the "alongside helper," to be a light and a guide to all believers. The presence of the Holy Spirit was then, among other things, a seal of approval and assurance that would be evident in the life of every believer. Ephesians 1:13 explains it: "In whom ye also trusted, after that ye heard the word of truth, the gospel of your salvation: in whom also after that ye believed, ye were sealed with that holy Spirit of promise." Ephesians 4:30 further instructs that we "grieve not the holy Spirit of God, whereby ye are sealed unto the day of redemption."

In Luke 3:22, we have been given a glorious picture of the nature of God that baffles the mind: "And the Holy Ghost descended in a bodily shape like a dove upon him, and a voice came from heaven, which said, Thou art my beloved Son; in thee I am well pleased."

Here we have the Father, the Holy Spirit and the Son being manifested all at the same time. The voice of the Father speaks (which proves God is still in heaven in some form), the Holy Spirit descends in the form of a dove (which proves that He is a witness of the Father's presence) and the Son (who is Immanuel, God with us) is approved by the Father. This is a great mystery! The Bible even calls it one. When Christ returns, we will all know how these three can be one. You can trust your whole salvation on the truth of God's word that says that these three are one and yet can operate separately, even if you can't conceive how this could be.

## What does the Bible teach about the "burning bosom"?

Mormons are thought that God reveals when something is true by causing our hearts to burn inside us when what we are asking, seeing, or hearing is from Him. They call this the, "Burning of the bosom". They are instructed to ask God in prayer if something is true and He will let them know in this way.

The only recorded event that comes close to this is found in Luke 24:32. "And they said one to another, Did not our heart burn within us, while he talked with us by the way, and while he opened to us the scriptures?"

This isn't a picture of someone asking a preconceived question and then getting an answer in the form of a burning bosom, as the Mormons use the term. Instead, it is the Lord, opening up the Word of God to them. As He explained the true meaning of the Word of God, the Lord confirmed it to their hearts. There is no record of this type of event being used by God to answer questions, especially about another gospel.

This burning bosom experience is the basis for many conversions to the Mormon faith. It was also the thing that plagued me most about leaving the church. When I was young, I had many burning bosom experiences. When I was delivered from the church, I wondered how that could be. The more I read from God's Word, however, the more I realized that the truth of God is not subject to our feelings.

Our feelings change, and sometimes our feelings are just wrong. We can be "at peace" about something and be way off base. I have felt this burning bosom feeling in many ways, and this alone would have kept me in the Mormon church if not for this one issue: I have felt a burning bosom feeling when asking about the Book of Mormon when I was younger, and again when asking if the church were true, and other times. But I have also felt the same burning bosom feeling—the peace, the warmth and joy—when asking if the Mormon church is a cult of the devil. Obviously, one of these extremes cannot true, and my point is this: the burning bosom is not sufficient to base the future of your soul and the souls of your loved ones on. It is the Word of God and its truthfulness alone upon which we can rely.

When the feelings and burning in my heart line up with the Word of God, I trust them. When they don't, I throw them out. If my heart burns within me and I can verify what it is saying with the Bible, I trust it. If it does not line up with the Bible, I no longer fear I have missed God.

Can Satan give us a feeling of peace? It's a typical Mormon question. So let's look at it. Yes, we can receive a false sense of peace from Satan. Matthew 7:22–23 says, "Many will say to me in that day, Lord, Lord, have we not prophesied in thy name? and in thy name have cast out devils? and in thy name done many wonderful works? And then will I profess unto them, I never knew you: depart from me, ye that work iniquity."

Here we see a group of people on the day of judgment who lived in complete confidence and peace that they were doing the works of God. Yet, Christ tells them, "I never knew you." As I have said before, if you are worshipping a Jesus who is not real, in the last day, you will never have known Him, and He will never have known you.

Even if Satan cannot give us feelings, we can generate feelings in our own hearts. We can deceive ourselves as this group mentioned above will have done.

The first Article of Faith sounds very Christian, yet, when Mormons say they believe in "God the eternal Father," they are talking about a different god, not the one of the Bible. When they say "and in His son, Jesus Christ," they do not speak of the promised Messiah "God with us" of the Bible. When they say "and in the Holy Ghost," it is not the Holy Ghost of the Bible.

It stands to reason then, that Mormons, while good, wonderful people, are not Christians as a whole, and they serve an altogether false God. The Bible clearly teaches it is not the "good" people who go to heaven, because none are good (Romans 3:10). It is, rather, those who believe in, trust in, rely on, and confess the true Messiah of the Word of God who will be saved (Romans 10:9–11).

## More on the Blasphemy against the Holy Ghost.

I want to make an important side note here in reference to the concept of blasphemy against the Holy Ghost. This is one of the most frightful things in the Bible to me. Without forgiveness, no one will see God, so who are these unfortunate ones with no hope of ever being forgiven? We've looked at Luke 12:10 already, so let's go to Hebrews 6:4–6.

"For it is impossible for those who were once enlightened, and have tasted of the heavenly gift, and were made partakers of the Holy Ghost, and have tasted the good word of God, and the powers of the world to come, if they shall fall away, to renew them again unto repentance; seeing they crucify to themselves the Son of God afresh, and put him to an open shame."

The Word of God says that if we confess our sins, God is faithful to forgive (1 John 1:9). With this fact in mind, I submit that the "seed" that is sown into the ground of our hearts by the Lord is always good. It is the ground, or the receiver, however, that God uses to produce the fruit if we are willing (Matthew 13:8). When a person hears the Word of God, the Holy Spirit witnesses the truthfulness of these words. Deep in the heart, he or she knows it is true. It may take many witnesses before this person really has the full understanding needed to choose to follow the truth. But if that person to whom God has fully shown His goodness and the goodness of His Word "falls away" from this truth by not receiving Christ as his Savior, he is rejecting the only source for salvation available. It is as if he has passively or even actively agreed with the crucifixion. That person is then "speaking against" the Holy Ghost who revealed this truth to him (or her).

When Jesus had produced every sign and wonder prophesied in the Torah, and the witness of the Spirit spoke from heaven, the people had all that they needed to make the choice to accept the Lord. They had tasted of all the "good word of God." They made a conscious choice to call all these witnesses evil and the Spirit, that of the devil. They rejected the only way to God.

Jesus, knowing their hearts, knew they would not repent of this, which made it an "unpardonable sin." This does not mean, however, that if a person has a weak and foolish moment and speaks evil of the Holy Ghost, they have no chance for forgiveness, nor does it mean that if one has been part of a false religion, they can never find forgiveness. This is only talking about those who are fully aware, who have all the witness of the truth, yet they completely reject the truth. They will receive no forgiveness in this life or the next, because they have made their choice to reject the only chance of redemption, rejecting the good seed all together. Notice in Matthew 13:8, mentioned above, that the plant grew in each case. Yet, depending on the soil or the cares of this life, it either took root or died out. We can be certain that those who deny the Holy Spirit will admit that the seed was good, and they knew it. They, too, will bow at the last day and confess with the devils—not unto salvation—that Jesus Christ is Lord.

# Chapter 6

## 2nd Article of Faith of the Church of Jesus Christ of Latter-day Saints

*Article 2. We believe that men will be punished for their own sins, and not for Adam's transgression.*

### What Mormons are taught about the sin of Adam.

The Mormon church teaches that the sin of Adam and Eve was a "wise" decision made first by Eve, then by Adam. They teach that procreation would not have been possible had they not seen the wisdom in disobeying God. This is expressed in The book of Moses {found in the LDS scripture called, the, Pearl of Great Price} 5:11: "And Eve, his wife, heard all these things and was glad, saying: Were it not for our transgression we never should have had seed, and never should have known good and evil, and the joy of our redemption, and the eternal life which God giveth unto all the obedient"

The LDS church mistakenly associates God's foreknowledge and desire to work all things to our good, with the idea that God crafted a plan that relies on our failures in order to work. But God's desire for mankind was for us to live in paradise with all our needs supplied forever. In fact, Adam and Eve already had eternal life supplied in the garden through the tree of life. Why would they think they would have to have to die in order to have eternal life? God's perfect will was for them to have a life of peace, beauty, and communion with Him.

Consider Luke 12:32. "Fear not, little flock; for it is your Father's good pleasure to give you the kingdom." It was never His desire that Adam should fall and suffer. He wanted to walk with them and bless them with everything He had created and had said was "very good" (Genesis 1:31).

He did know they would fall, however, and He prepared for that. As the Bible says, Jesus was "slain from the foundation of the world" (Luke 11:50).

Why then would God make a tree that could bring death? To understand this, it's important to understand the power of our freedom of choice. If death is not an option, then it is impossible to choose life for ourselves. Without this option, we are, as the world likes to say, just another animal. But we are *not* just another animal. We have been created in the image of an all-powerful God. All living creatures are not in the same category as mere animals, whose only option is to follow their natural instincts. First Corinthians 15:39 clearly states, "All flesh is not the same flesh: but there is one kind of flesh of men, another flesh of beasts, another of fishes, and another of birds."

The Lord made us—mankind—to be free. Without options, there is no freedom. Without freedom, there can be no real love for God. The Mormons don't really disagree with this point; however, I mention it to illustrate the fact that it was not God's will that Adam and Eve should go this way, but the option had to be there. They had life (the tree of life) on one hand and death (the tree of the knowledge of good and evil) on the other. The Lord was saying in essence, as He later did to the children of Israel in Deuteronomy 30:19–20, "I call heaven and earth to record this day against you, that I have set before you life and death, blessing and cursing: therefore choose life, that both thou and thy seed may live: That thou mayest love the LORD thy God, and that thou mayest obey his voice, and that thou mayest cleave unto him: for he is thy life."

Clearly, God's desire was for mankind to choose life and peace, as it always will be.

Genesis 3:16–19 also makes it clear that the fall was nothing to rejoice over, but rather, a cause of great sorrow.

"Unto the woman he said, I will greatly multiply thy sorrow and thy conception; in sorrow thou shalt bring forth children; and thy desire shall be to thy husband, and he shall rule over thee. And unto Adam he said, Because thou hast hearkened unto the voice of thy wife, and hast eaten of the tree, of which I commanded thee, saying, Thou shalt not eat of it: cursed is the ground for thy sake; in sorrow shalt thou eat of it all the days of thy life; Thorns also and thistles shall it bring forth to thee; and thou shalt eat the herb of the field; In the sweat of thy face shalt thou eat bread, till thou return unto the ground; for out of it wast thou taken: for dust thou art, and unto dust shalt thou return."

God's plans can never be stopped. Knowing all things, the Lord had already constructed a plan of redemption for mankind (to buy us back from sin) by sending Messiah (the Savior) through their own lineage to cover for this and all resulting sin. This foreknowledge of knowing all possible scenarios and making preparation for them is not the same as God's perfect will. God, in His mercy, covered their nakedness (the awareness of their sin) with a slain animal's skin (Genesis 3:21). In the same way, Jesus was slain for the covering of sin from the very foundation of time.

## The Bible does not imply Adam and Eve were unable to have children before they sinned.

Another great misconception of the Mormon doctrine is that somehow Adam and Eve could not have children unless they were aware of sin by partaking of the fruit. The Bible does not teach, in any way, this concept. God created them, like all other creatures of earth, to have seed within themselves. It is against the nature of God to set up a situation that if they had not sinned, they would not have been able to have children. If they were unable to have children before the fall, God would not have commanded them to "be fruitful and multiply and replenish the earth" before the fall (Genesis 1:28).

God is not in the tempting business. He does not use sin to fulfill His purposes. "Let no man say when he is tempted, I am tempted of God: for God cannot be tempted with evil, neither tempteth he any man" (James 1:13). God is able, however, to turn even the worst situation to our good.

The truth is that Adam and Eve just hadn't had children before they had sinned. They were in a world free of the constant pressure we face to have sex. They were created into a state of immortality with no rush to begin a family. Adam and Eve were busy tending to the garden and getting to know each other. It wasn't until Adam truly "knew" his wife that they conceived. This was not a sinful act, as the Mormons imply. Nor was the fact that, at the time they fell, they had not yet had children.

## How long did it take before children were born in Adam's time?

There is no mention of how long Adam and Eve were in the garden before they sinned; it could have been many, many years. If you look closely at the genealogies stated in Genesis, it was common for people of the day to wait over a hundred years before having a first child. One example of this is found in Genesis 5:18: "And Jared lived an hundred sixty and two years, and he begat Enoch."

Thus, as part of the curse, Eve would still bring forth the same children she would have, but now it would be involve pain and labor rather instead of being a peaceful event. This fact, however, does not mean that she was previously unable to have children at all, as the Mormons are told.

In the same way, Adam didn't first begin to work the ground of the garden after he sinned. Nor did he only begin to eat bread after the fall. Instead, he would now discover that what had once been a pleasant event had now become much more difficult. What was once done with the joy of walking with the Lord was now done in sorrow and pain.

## What the Mormon church means by the concept of not being punished for Adam's transgression.

At its core, this statement is a denial of the sin nature that brings every human face to face with the need for the cross of Christ. Joseph Smith taught his followers that it is because we sin ourselves—and though we can achieve holiness through "obedience" but won't—that we need Jesus. According to this thinking, our need of salvation does not come because we are all fallen by nature and sinful from birth, as stated in the Bible.

This nature is evident in the smallest child who, unaware of right and wrong, pulls away from her parents in rebellious defiance at every turn. The very act of learning discipline is to learn how to control this sinful nature that lies within us all.

Joseph Smith taught that mankind is born into a sinless state. In a Mormon's understanding, all children, whether of believers or unbelievers, are pure, and in God's eyes, perfect, without the sin nature until they first understand and then commit sin. Theologically, they deal with the death of children by performing vicarious baptisms for these deceased children in their temples. (They also believe that no one will go to heaven who has not been baptized in water.) We will discuss the mercy of God toward children and those unaware of sin and therefore not under it later. Suffice it to say, at this point, that God does not send babies to hell if they die before they get baptized.

## Mormons are not taught to believe that the sin nature that Adam passed on in the flesh is a thing to be repented of; nor do they believe that it separates us from God, in and of itself.

Mormons are taught that Adam's sin had bearing upon us only in that we, too, are now subject to physical death because of it. Allow me to give you an illustration in my own words here. This is an example from my understanding, not theirs. It is, however, the implication of their teaching.

In a Mormon's understanding of the sin nature, it is as if you have a bank account of sorts. Your account starts out full of goodness. As you grow older and become more aware of sin, you begin to sin, and you draw upon that account of goodness. If you don't put goodness back into your account through good deeds, ordinances (baptism, etc.), and works, your sins will outweigh your personal holiness. If this is not corrected, you will not be found worthy to go to heaven. This is because (they are taught), grace only saves you "after all you can do." You must achieve a certain, somewhat undefined, level of personal holiness in order to be saved. I say "undefined" because while they must perform all the rites of membership and marriage in the temple and such, they have no assurance of salvation in this life until they are judged. There's more to their beliefs, as I said; I give this merely as an illustration. We will discuss the Mormon concept of salvation shortly.

## What the Bible teaches about the sin of Adam and what it means to us.

The Bible teaches that the sin of Adam and Eve came about because they accepted the lies Satan told them. Satan's primary cookie that he waved before them was they could become as gods, knowing good and evil. It wasn't their desire to have children that caused them to sin, as the Mormons are taught. Rather, it was the desire to become as gods that motivated them. They saw it as a way to become wise in order to be like gods, not as a means of doing God's will. What a sinful thought—to think that God would give a command that could only be followed if another one were disobeyed. It's repulsive.

As stated in early chapters, this was the same desire that Satan had had himself. The same desire that caused the expulsion of him and his followers from the presence of the Father in heaven, got Adam and Eve expelled from the Garden and separated from God's presence as well. That separation brought about spiritual death.

## The Bible teaches that when Adam sinned, it not only brought physical death to all, but "spiritual death" (separation from the presence of God) for all mankind.

All sin brings corruption or death of both body and spirit. Therefore, the only sins "not unto death" are those sins that have been repented of and that are covered by the blood of Christ's sacrifice. Even in the natural, however, there is always some form of death that occurs when we keep sinning. Consider James 1:15. "Then when lust hath conceived, it bringeth forth sin: and sin, when it is finished, bringeth forth death." This is a serious problem that, if left uncorrected, would forever separate all mankind from the Father who is life.

Romans 5:12 says, "Wherefore, as by one man sin entered into the world, and death by sin; and so death passed upon all men, for that all have sinned." When Adam sinned, he brought corruption into a perfect environment. Corruption has no power to bring forth or birth anything but corruption. This is why we are all "born into sin."

Matthew 7:17–18 explains that, "even so every good tree bringeth forth good fruit; but a corrupt tree bringeth forth evil fruit. A good tree cannot bring forth evil fruit, neither can a corrupt tree bring forth good fruit." When Adam sinned, his very nature became sinful—his way of thinking, his desires, his thoughts, all became evil and corrupted. The sin nature was in his flesh and would be passed on to all mankind through his blood.

In Romans 8:7, we read "Because the carnal mind is enmity against God: for it is not subject to the law of God, neither indeed can be." The nature of man became carnal, sensual, and full of sin. This sin forever would have separated us from God. "But your iniquities have separated between you and your God, and your sins have hid his face from you, that he will not hear"

(Isaiah 59:2). This is not a state that we can get ourselves out of by our actions because the Word of God says in Romans 3:10, "As it is written, there is none righteous, no, not one."

## God is not unjust. He has no desire to punish others for the sin of their fathers (Adam's transgression).

When sin entered into the world, all flesh and creation became subject to a corrupted state. Sin entered into the world by Adam and was passed to all. Consider Romans 8:20–22.

"For the creature was made subject to vanity, not willingly, but by reason of him who hath subjected the same in hope, because the creature itself also shall be delivered from the bondage of corruption into the glorious liberty of the children of God. For we know that the whole creation groaneth and travaileth in pain together until now."

In other words, this corruption and death are hereditary. I often hear those who blame God for the death of a newborn. This comes from a lack of understanding of consequences. We are always free to choose what we will do for the most part. Yet, we are never free to choose the consequences of these choices. For example, if I choose to do illegal intravenous drugs, I may contract AIDS. If I then have a child, there is a good chance that child will also contract AIDS and possibly die. It was my choice—not God's hand—that caused or at least contributed to this death. It was not the action of some angry God, nor does it reflect a lack of compassion on His part. The child received the results of the corruption of my flesh by no fault of his/her own.

## If I do not repent and except Jesus as my Savior before I die, I may also be accountable for the sins of those influenced by my failure to teach the truth I know.

Many people throughout our history have deliberately taught their children to do evil. If these children grow up with no opportunity to hear the good news of God's salvation, the sins of this child will then pass to the guilty party who willfully taught them to sin. This is, incidentally, the same as failing to teach them the truth when we know it.

In the same way, when Adam and Eve made a choice to disobey God by eating that which was forbidden, their actions brought corruption into not only their blood, but the blood of the whole world. Their tainted blood brought a curse to all creation that has been passed on to each generation. God has no choice but to pronounce all creation unjust (imperfect).

Apart from the work of Christ, no flesh would see God—not even a child or a person mentally challenged to the point of being incapable of understanding. However, the grace of God is able to cover such things, because the Bible teaches that where there is no law, there is no sin. The sin nature is covered in such cases and either justified (by the faith of the believing parent) or held to the account of the fathers who first brought the evil by denying the salvation of God through faith in the Messiah. In other cases, the blood of the sinners is held to the account of the people entrusted with the truth who yet do not warn their children or their neighbors.

Ezekiel 3:18 says, "When I say unto the wicked, Thou shalt surely die; and thou givest him not warning, nor speakest to warn the wicked from his wicked way, to save his life; the same wicked man shall die in his iniquity; but his blood will I require at thine hand."

Another example of others being held accountable for the sin of others is found in Matthew 23:35–36: "That upon you may come all the righteous blood shed upon the earth, from the blood of righteous Abel unto the blood of Zacharias son of Barachias, whom ye slew between the temple and the altar. Verily I say unto you, All these things shall come upon this generation."

Here we see that the innocent blood spilt was made chargeable to a certain generation of sinners in Christ's time—a people so evil they denied the Lord, even after having seen for themselves the power, the witness, and the proof that He was, indeed, the promised Messiah.

## The Bible teaches that the children of believers are covered.

The blood of Christ covers the innocent who die. First Corinthians 7:14 tells us that "the unbelieving husband is sanctified by the wife, and the unbelieving wife is sanctified by the husband: else were your children unclean; but now are they holy." This scripture makes it clear that a believer's child who dies is covered by the faith of their believing parent, at least until they are old enough to understand for themselves and accept or reject the gift of salvation.

I do not pretend to have a full understanding of how this mystery works; however, one thing I know, and of this I am certain. God has worked it out.

While God will not send a child to hell for Adam's transgression or the sin nature, we are all made sinners because of it. We must understand that God's mercy far exceeds our understanding of how this will all work. No one will be able to say at the last day that God's judgments are not just. Every knee, both the righteous and unrighteous, both saved and the lost, will bow and confess that Jesus is the Christ, and that God's ways were just and holy and right.

Would it not be impossible to call God just and right and good if babies were consigned to hell for someone else's sin? To be cast into hell as a baby for not being baptized? I would never serve, nor call holy, a being who would do such a thing.

All sin must be punished by death. That death will either be the death of Christ on the cross on our behalf, or the blood of those that reject His free gift and teach others to do so as well.

# Chapter 7

## The Third Article of Faith of the Church of Jesus Christ of Latter-day Saints

*Article 3. We believe that through the atonement of Christ, all mankind may be saved, by obedience to the laws and ordinances of the Gospel.*

## The Mormon Concept of Salvation and How to Achieve It

Mormons are taught that salvation is only possible because of Jesus Christ, but this salvation can only be accessed "after all you can do." Because of this and other teachings, Mormons do not see the word *salvation* as Christians do. According to their theology, they cannot know for sure that they are "saved."

From the Christian standpoint, to be saved includes and gives us full access to all that God has to offer. This assurance is gained upon confession and a true belief from the heart that causes a real change that brings right living in the new believer's life. This change, however, is the sovereign result of the work of the Holy Spirit, not the efforts of the new Christian.

In contrast, the only way Mormons can know that they are completely saved from death and hell is to have such a high level of personal holiness as to have a personal revelation by God that reveals to them that their "calling and election is made sure." A revelation reserved for only those who have attained to a very high, or near perfect life. They will have passed every possible test that God has placed before them.

# Mormons do not seek for salvation, but rather, "exultation".

Mormons are taught that we are spirits born in heaven then placed on earth to gain a body. This life was a gift of God to mankind so that we too could gain a body and hopefully experience a "fullness of joy" as God does. For a Mormon, life is a series of tests that God puts us through to teach us and to find out if we are willing to keep all of His commandments and ordinances.

Thus, salvation is not what a Mormon is seeking. For a Mormon, salvation (as understood by a Christian) is only the beginning of the journey. Being saved is not to be with God in heaven, but only the escaping of the death sentence that was pronounced upon Adam and his seed as a consequence of his sin. They are taught that everyone will be saved from this death and stand before God to be judged because of Jesus's sacrifice. To them, this is the end of salvation.

Instead of salvation, a Mormon is taught to seek exaltation. This is a state in which a person has obeyed all of God's laws to the best of their ability, and has performed all the ordinances they are taught to follow. After a Mormon is judged and found worthy by God, they can then hope to be exalted to a state in which they will progress in their priesthood to the office or calling of godhood. At that point, they will be able to have spirit children by procreation with one of many wives and become gods of their own worlds.

This is a concept known to them as "eternal progression." This thinking follows the logic that if we are children of God, we naturally will one day grow up to be gods too—if we pass all the tests along the way.

# According to Mormon teaching, what is "obedience to the laws and ordinances of the gospel"?

According to Mormon teaching, a faithful member of the church must do all of the following (and more) in order to be with God the Father in the third heaven.

1.  They must be baptized as a member of the church by a person given authority by God. In order to be baptized, a person must first repent of all the wrongdoings of your life (as defined by the church), and agree to strive to never do them again.

Believers must follow not only the biblical ten commandments but other standards of living as defined by their prophets, one of which is called "the word of wisdom." The word of wisdom is a set of rules given, supposedly by God, that each penitent person should follow. Some of these rules include abstaining from "hot drinks" such as tea and coffee, abstaining from smoking or the use of tobacco of any kind, and abstaining from drinking any alcohol or anything containing caffeine. In addition, followers are instructed to practice abstinence of all immorality of dress and action, to name a few.

2.  They must receive the gift of the Holy Ghost by the laying on of the hands of the authorized leaders or elders of the church.

3.  If male, they receive the priesthood by the laying on of the hands of the authorized leaders or elders of the church. If female, they are to be married to a holder of the priesthood in a Mormon temple by the authorized leaders elders or high priests of the church. The temple marriage is considered to be in force for time and all eternity. In order to be exalted and be with God, a member must be "sealed" to his/her mate in the temple and remain faithful to God until death.

In a temple marriage, certain ordinances are performed, including sealing ordinances, baptisms for the dead, washings, and endowments. These are done first for the prospective couple and then for the ancestors of the couple who may not have had a chance to hear the Mormon teachings while still alive.

The marriage itself takes a good part of a day, but the proxy work for their family takes years and is a process that faithful members will be engaged in for the rest of their lives with as much time as they have to offer.

The belief is that if a person did not do these things while alive, they are sent to a "spirit prison." In this prison, they are given the chance to receive the ordinances mentioned above. The living members of the church perform these ordinances on behalf of the dead by standing in proxy for the deceased. In other words, a living person must do them on their behalf. They, the dead, are then given the chance to be released from this prison if they accept these ordinances as if they had done them in the flesh themselves.

This is why the Mormon church has the most extensive genealogy system in the world. They believe that by the time Jesus returns, every person that has ever lived will have had a chance to be baptized, and all the ordinances performed on their behalf by a living relative.

It is beyond the purpose and scope of this book to address the full temple services and all that they mean to a Mormon member. In short, however, in order to be worthy to go to the temples, Mormons must profess to be keeping all the commandments as understood by them, and to be paying ten percent of their income in tithing. They must verbally acknowledge their belief in Joseph Smith as a true prophet and that the church is the only true church on earth. They must state their belief in the current modern prophet as the only authorized representative of Jesus Christ, as well as the current leadership of the church. They must also give account for their amount of service to the local church in "visiting teaching" by females and "home teaching" by males. In addition, other acts of giving and service are needed in order to receive a "temple recommend" from their local bishop. This recommend must be renewed regularly in order to ensure that the individuals remain faithful to the Mormon doctrine. Couples often serve full time in the temple upon retirement.

### *Returning to the discussion of the requirements of Exaltation.*

4.  A member in good standing must pay a full tithe of ten percent, plus they must fast and donate the money they would have

used to buy their meal, to the poor. This happens at "fasting and testimony meetings," which occur the first Sunday of each month.

5.  As stated earlier, members must keep all of the commandments of God as well as those that have been passed down by the leadership of the church on behalf of God.

6.  Members must testify to a belief in God the Eternal Father, and in His Son, Jesus Christ and that Joseph Smith was a true prophet; along with all the subsequent prophets since that time.

7.  If at all possible, every male must go on a two-year mission upon reaching the age of at least nineteen and having been ordained an elder.

8.  Females, at the age of twenty-one, are encouraged to go on missions as well. Females do not receive the priesthood in the Mormon faith.

9.  Members must read from their scriptures and express a belief in all the standard works of scriptures of the church. These consist of: the Book of Mormon, the Doctrine and Covenants, the Pearl of Great Price, and lastly, the Bible, which they believe to be of lesser value due to mistranslation.

10. Members must specifically express belief that the Book of Mormon is the word of God.

There are other requirements, but this is an outline of the main ones. All of these ordinances, as well as the Ten Commandments, must be fulfilled in order to be with God the Father, His Son Jesus Christ, and the Holy Ghost in heaven.

## The Three Degrees of Heaven

According to Mormon perspective, salvation is only a starting point. Mormons are taught that heaven is segregated into what is known as the three degrees of heaven or the three degrees of glory.

A summary of this belief is that all persons who reject the Mormon gospel on earth will go to the lowest place in heaven, known as the telestial kingdom. In this kingdom, they will not be allowed to be married or to enjoy the presence of Jesus or the Father.

Persons who received the Lord as Savior but did not believe the Mormon gospel, such as faithful traditional Christians and those who were not baptized into the church but who led a good life will go to a place in heaven known as the terrestrial kingdom. In this is kingdom, a person will not be able to be married, but will enjoy the presence of Jesus Christ and the Holy Ghost, but not God the Father. Remember that in their understanding, these are three completely different people.

The third or highest degree of glory, or heaven, is known as the celestial kingdom. This honor is reserved only for Mormons who kept all the commandments and ordinances mentioned above. Those members who receive this glory will dwell with God the Father, Jesus Christ, and the Holy Ghost. They will remain married for all time to the spouse they had on earth. Males will also receive many additional wives for the purpose of procreation. They are taught that these marriages will produce spirit children who will then start the process over again with them as head of a new world of their own, reigning as gods. Their world will have a new Adam and Eve, a new Savior, and perhaps an only begotten son like Jesus was to God etc. Of course, one wonders how this could be if they had ever had children before. How would this be their "only begotten?" However, this aspect of eternal progression is not made clear and is not a major teaching topic one might hear at services.

[Continuing with the topic the Mormon view of heaven]

Those who reject the Mormon teachings on earth—as well as Satan and his followers and demons—will receive no glory but will be cast into a place known as "outer darkness." This is a place in which the soul will dwell for the rest of eternity, alone and in darkness. Mormons do not believe that hell will be a place of fire, but rather a place where the pain of separation from God will be as a fire in the heart that will never be quenched.

## What the Bible Teaches about Salvation

The Bible teaches us that because Adam sinned, this brought sin upon all that came after. Romans 5:15–16 says:

"But not as the offence, so also is the free gift. For if through the offence of one many be dead, much more the grace of God, and the gift by grace, which is by one man, Jesus Christ, hath abounded unto many. And not as it was by one that sinned, so is the gift: for the judgment was by one to condemnation, but the free gift is of many offences unto justification."

Please note that the death that was brought on by Adam was more than a physical death. It also brought condemnation. No one is ever worthy to go to heaven. The Bible states in Romans 3:10, "As it is written, There is none righteous, no, not one." Even our best efforts are considered unclean, defiled things. Isaiah 64:6 says, "But we are all as a unclean thing, and all our righteousnesses are as filthy rags: and we all do fade as a leaf; and our iniquities, like the wind, have taken us away."

This is why Romans 3:23 says, "For all have sinned, and come short of the glory of God." We are all sinners and fall short of God's holy standard. None of us can ever become holy by our own efforts because even our righteousness (good deeds) are defiled in the eyes of a holy God. Because of this sinfulness, we have earned the sentence that God pronounced in the Garden—Death.

As Romans 6:23 tells us, "the wages of sin is death; but the gift of God is eternal life through Jesus Christ our Lord." If the wages of sin is death, then in order for sin to be atoned for, it is necessary that a life be given. A wage is something you earn, "but the gift of God is eternal life." You don't earn gifts. When your birthday comes, you don't go to your parents and say "I've achieved another year of life; now give me the gift I have earned for being born."

Your birth is a gift you have no way to earn. In the same way, your spiritual birth in Christ is not something you can earn. It is a free gift of God. Eternal life is not something to be attained by achievement or the keeping of ordinances and righteousness; it is a free gift of God. God, in His mercy, remembers we are but dust. See Psalm 103:14—"For he knoweth our frame; he remembereth that we are dust." He has made a way for us to be redeemed from this death we earned by sinning.

In the days before Christ, God instituted a system of atonement that was a foreshadowing of the ultimate atonement of a perfect life. But it was not possible that the blood of goats and bulls could fully atone for sin. Hebrews 9:9 says that this sacrifice "was a figure for the time then present, in which were offered both gifts and sacrifices, that could not make him that did the service perfect, as pertaining to the conscience."

The concept of redemption comes from the law of the near-of-kin redeemer, as expressed in Leviticus 25:47–49. According to that law, if a person sold himself into slavery, a close family relative could buy him back and free him from the bondage. If the person who had sold himself had the money to pay, he could also buy himself back or redeem himself. Here is the text:

"And if a sojourner or stranger wax rich by thee, and thy brother that dwelleth by him wax poor, and sell himself unto the stranger or sojourner by thee, or to the stock of the stranger's family: After that he is sold he may be redeemed again; one of his brethren may redeem him: Either his uncle, or his uncle's son, may redeem him, or any that is nigh of kin unto him of his family may redeem him; or if he be able, he may redeem himself."

As stated earlier, we earned the wages of death by our sin. We are, therefore, slaves to the sin nature. We not only have sold ourselves to sin but continue to do so with every new infraction or omission. Galatians 3:10: "For as many as are of the works of the law are under the curse: for it is written, Cursed is every one that continueth not in all things which are written in the book of the law to do them." Therefore, with each new sin, we encore a new sin debt.

Romans 7:14 says, "For we know that the law is spiritual: but I am carnal, sold under sin." All of our earthy relatives have also sold themselves by sinning. In fact, we all keep reselling ourselves back into slavery. Because of this, neither we nor our relatives could ever have the ability to redeem ourselves or anyone else.

Jesus is the only one who lived a sinless life and who, therefore, did not owe a sin debt of His own. This is why He is known as our redeemer. To redeem is to buy back. Where we sold ourselves into sin, Christ has offered to buy us back. If we accept this, Christ becomes our redeemer and our master who literally owns us. But in this, we can rejoice.

**Job 19:25**: For I know that my redeemer liveth, and that he shall stand at the latter day upon the earth.

**Psalm 19:14:** Let the words of my mouth, and the meditation of my heart, be acceptable in thy sight, O Lord, my strength, and my redeemer.

**The ordinances were a shadow and a type of things to come.**
**Colossians 2:14:** Blotting out the handwriting of ordinances that was against us, which was contrary to us, and took it out of the way, nailing it to his cross.

**Colossians 2:20:** Wherefore if ye be dead with Christ from the rudiments of the world, why, as though living in the world, are ye subject to ordinances,

The "ordinances of the gospel" were a type of greater things to come. They were not the actual means of access to God, but a type of the redemption of Christ for mankind.

**Ephesians 2:15:** Having abolished in his flesh the enmity, even the law of commandments contained in ordinances; for to make in himself of twain one new man, so making peace.

**Hebrews 9:1:** Then verily the first covenant had also ordinances of divine service, and a worldly sanctuary.

**Hebrews 9:10:** Which stood only in meats and drinks, and divers washings, and carnal ordinances, imposed on them until the time of reformation.

The purpose of the temple and the ordinances were to gain access to God's blessings as a result of forgiveness of sin. Jesus's sacrifice of His sinless life was the perfect sacrifice they were all looking for. When this sacrifice was performed, both the law and the ordinances were fulfilled.

## The temple service was not a secretive mystery.

The temple was not a secret mystery with marriages and such being performed. Everything from the dimensions of the structure, the purpose, the exact furniture inside, all were clearly set forth. Even the type of sacrifices, who would do them and why; what the "seas" (ceremonial wash basins) were for, and every detail was clearly set forth in scripture. Rest assured that when Hebrews 9:5 says, "and over it the cherubims of glory shadowing the mercyseat; of which we cannot now speak particularly," it is hardly evidence that the temple ordinances and activities were a secret as the Mormons teach. Yet I have heard this verse quoted many times as proof that the temple was, as Joseph Smith claimed, a place of secret oaths and endowments.

I see even less proof—zero—that marriages were performed there.

It is so important to note that the whole claim of the Mormon church is that it is a restoration of the original, biblical church. The Bible clearly defines what went on in its temples. What is not mentioned in reference to temples, and what did not happen, were baptisms for the dead, marriages, females being led through the veil by their husbands, secret oaths and death promises for revealing the secrets. There were no signs and symbols that act out the different ways one would die if the covenants were broken or secrets revealed. These are all things from the secret society of the Free Masons, not the hand of God.

We will talk more about the temples with the discussion of the makeup of the church leadership in the sixth Article of Faith.

When Jesus fulfilled the law with His perfect sacrifice, He paid the ransom for all who would receive this free gift. All the reasons for having a temple were fulfilled in Christ at that time. Christ prophesied that the temple would be destroyed and a new one "built without hands" would take its place. This was a reference to the body of Christ.

Yet, according to the teachings of Joseph Smith, salvation as we know it is only attained because of the temple. This is because exaltation (what a Christian calls salvation) is said by Mormons to be only for those who are sealed in the temples. In this way, the Mormon church has, in effect, placed their temple ordinances above the atonement of Christ; because it is only by them that one would be with God. Jesus said, however, in John 14:6, "I am the way, the truth, and the life: no man cometh unto the Father, but by me."

Therefore, the only way to God—to be in His sheepfold and later inherit all that He has—is through Jesus Christ and his redemption, not through temple marriage or any other way (see John 10:1).

# Chapter 8

## Continuation of the Third Article of Faith

*Article 3. We believe that through the atonement of Christ, all mankind may be saved, by obedience to the laws and ordinances of the Gospel.*

## How Does Someone "Receive Christ"?

**John 3:3:** Jesus answered and said unto him, Verily, verily, I say unto thee, Except a man be born again, he cannot see the kingdom of God.

**John 1:12:** But as many as received him, to them gave he power to become the sons of God, even to them that believe on his name:

When a person receives the death of Christ as payment of their sin, the Lord Himself gives them the power to become sons (and, of course, daughters). It is not something we do, but something we receive.

In John 3:3, we learn that we must be "born again" from above in order to see God. We are born again by receiving the Holy Spirit when Jesus becomes our Savior. We become a new creation, never before in existence, and we are filled with the Holy Spirit. We are freed from the grip of sin in our spirits and are justified by the blood of Christ as though we never had sinned. Consider Romans 10:9–11.

"If thou shalt confess with thy mouth the Lord Jesus, and shalt believe in thine heart that God hath raised him from the dead, thou shalt be saved. For with the heart man believeth unto righteousness; and with the mouth confession is made unto salvation. For the scripture saith, Whosoever believeth on him shall not be ashamed."

Salvation in the kingdom of God in all its glory is a free gift that need only be asked for, believed in and received.

The scripture is plain and pure: salvation comes from true confession alone. A Mormon or others who do not understand the grace of God will scream "what about the need for keeping the commandments?" and "Faith without works is dead." Let's look back at these verses for the answer to these great questions. Notice in verse 9 that confession is only half of the verse. The second half deals with belief. If a person truly believes from the heart that God raised Jesus from the dead, this belief will produce right living, or righteousness, from the heart. If this transformation is not evident in that person's life, you can be sure that this person is not really a believer. It is, however, for God to judge. You can confess the right things all day long—"Jesus is the son of God"—just as the devils do, but if it isn't a belief of conviction from the heart that leads unto righteousness, it doesn't save you. If it did, the devils would also be saved at the end when, as Philippians 2:10–11 reminds us, every knee will bow and every tongue will confess that Jesus Christ is Lord.

Regardless of this fact however, as Romans 10:9–11 explains above, confession is made unto salvation. The salvation is not a result of the righteousness. The righteousness is a result of the salvation. This is the "work" of salvation—to believe. Second Timothy 1:9 says it is the Lord "who hath saved us, and called us with an holy calling, not according to our works, but according to his own purpose and grace, which was given us in Christ Jesus before the world began."

Abraham believed God, and it was accounted unto him as righteousness. In the same way, if we believe that God sent His Son and raised Him from the dead for our sins, we will be accounted as righteous by this faith alone, as was Abraham. We are then saved—forever. This is the work of Abraham's faith: he believed, so he acted. The action, or works, were a result of the faith he had. He believed, so he picked up the knife. The righteousness was only because of, and a result of, his faith alone.

Ephesians 2:8–10 says it is "by grace are ye saved through faith; and that not of yourselves: it is the gift of God: not of works, lest any man should boast. For we are his workmanship, created in Christ Jesus unto good works, which God hath before ordained that we should walk in them." The works do not save us nor qualify us, they are merely evidence of the grace (empowering presence of God) in our lives. James said it this way, "Yea, a man may say, Thou hast faith, and I have works: shew me thy faith without thy works, and I will shew thee my faith by my works" (James 2:18). Jesus Himself said in John 3:16, "For God so loved the world, that he gave his only begotten Son, that whosoever believeth in him should not perish, but have everlasting life."

A true confession is one in which a person expresses faith (belief) in Jesus as the risen Son of God from the heart. This belief leads to righteousness (works) for anyone who truly believes. But it is not these works that bring salvation. Salvation comes to whosoever believes and confesses.

This unearned grace or justification (to be accounted as just and holy before God) comes only by the will of the Father. When we stand before Him uncondemned, we will not be able to say "Lord, I know it was by Your grace that I'm here in heaven, but I did all I could do to help You out." We who are saved will know it was God who gave us both the desire (He is the author) and the ability (He is the finisher) to be saved, not by our efforts. Hebrews 12:2 explains that Jesus is "the author and finisher of our faith; who for the joy that was set before him endured the cross, despising the shame, and is set down at the right hand of the throne of God."

When we accept the salvation Christ offers, we are presented to God as holy and unblameable, beyond reproof. We are no longer subject to the old Law, but a higher law of grace. Colossians 1:22 says that he has reconciled us "in the body of his flesh through death, to present you holy and unblameable and unreproveable in his sight."

## How should we live after we receive salvation?

From a biblical perspective, we learn that salvation or justification—being called just and holy by God—comes the minute we truly accept Jesus's free gift. There is, however, a second process that begins after one is saved, which can take a lifetime, or as long it takes for us to surrender our will over to the Lord. This process is called sanctification.

Sanctification is a process through which God Himself helps us to work out the transformation that has taken place within our spirit, into the flesh. To be sanctified is to be "set aside for holy use." With each situation of life comes a choice. We can set aside our will, our emotions, and our minds for holy use and be highly blessed, or we can hold back parts that we don't want to surrender and suffer for our choices. The problem with not submitting to His will is that God makes that a very uncomfortable choice. God Himself blesses us when we submit an area of our lives and lovingly corrects us when we don't. He loves us too much to do nothing to correct our wanderings and evil acts. This correction, while painful to the believer, brings the fruits of sanctification and maturity.

Again, if we truly belong to God, we will suffer this correction from time to time. It's not fun, but it always produces a closer walk if we submit to it; and in the end, God always works it out to be a blessing, no matter how much it may hurt at the time. "For whom the Lord loveth he chasteneth, and scourgeth every son whom he receiveth" (Hebrews 12:6).

## Holy living is not optional for the Christian.

The Bible teaches that after we receive salvation, we should strive for a life of holiness. This is a life that is not marked so much by living a list of do's and don'ts as much as a life that is considered to no longer be ours to do with what we choose.

The Bible calls this "walking in the Spirit." We know we are walking in or with the Spirit when we are focused more on communication with the Father and the things of God than dealing with the flesh.

Many people seem to have their focus all out of whack—I know I did for years. I focused all my efforts on trying to do right, to be a good person. What this did was put the focus all on me. I was living to make sure I did right, that I changed myself, that I was holy. I found a wonderful freedom, however, when I stopped focusing on my ability to do right and put all that effort into walking with the Lord. I learned to focus on keeping my thoughts under His control, on taking every thought that was in opposition to His Word—all my doubts, fears, lusts, and so on—and replacing them with something right and true and pure.

This a daily thing, a daily choice and focus. Admittedly, some days are better than others. However, I no longer walk around in guilt and shame, because my life is not mine to condemn. The truth is, I am guilty. I do deserve to be punished. I have wrong thoughts, ideas, and motives at times, but I am washed; I am free. My life is not mine to condemn or repair but to sanctify, to set apart for holy use. Truly, this battlefield is in my mind. I no longer live to repair myself, but I spend my time just seeking for more of the Lord in my heart. The wonderful thing is the freedom from the desire for sin this has given me. I find that I no longer have as much of a desire for the things I once struggled with. I find that the more I'm focused on the Lord, the less I walk in the flesh and the lusts of my old ways. Second Corinthians 5:15 says that "he died for all, that they which live should not henceforth live unto themselves, but unto him which died for them, and rose again." Our lives have been paid for—as we were once slaves to sin, we are to consider ourselves as slaves to righteousness.

Many have brought shame and reproach on the faith by living a lifestyle of the world while claiming the cross of Christ. The Bible clearly states however that we are to shun sin. Romans 6:1–6 says:

"What shall we say then? Shall we continue in sin, that grace may abound? God forbid. How shall we, that are dead to sin, live any longer therein? Know ye not, that so many of us as were baptized into Jesus Christ were baptized into his death? Therefore we are buried with him by baptism into death: that like as Christ was raised up from the dead by the glory of the Father, even so we also should walk in newness of life. For if we have been planted together in the likeness of his death, we shall be also in the likeness of his resurrection: knowing this, that our old man is crucified with him, that the body of sin might be destroyed, that henceforth we should not serve sin."

James 2:12 warns us we should speak and act and live as those that will be judged by the law. In other words, we are to live our lives as if we were going to be judged by the law, even though we are free from it and it is liberty to us, not bondage.

## How long does salvation last?

If you have a child you will understand, as I have come to, that no matter what a child does, he or she will always be your child. Your child may do many things to upset you, but nothing he or you can do will ever make that child stop being your flesh and blood, your child.

Even if you don't want the child, even if it dies, it is still your child. How much less would God be able to undo the work of salvation in our lives in which we become "sons of God" (John 1:12).

Nothing you can do, nothing anyone else can do, *nothing* can take us too high or too low to stop being the beloved children of God once we are truly born again into His family. Romans 8:35–39 states this clearly.

"Who shall separate us from the love of Christ? Shall tribulation, or distress, or persecution, or famine, or nakedness, or peril, or sword? Nor height, nor depth, nor any other creature, shall be able to separate us from the love of God, which is in Christ Jesus our Lord."

Don't worry, there's much more—John 10:28 says "I give unto them eternal life; and they shall never perish, neither shall any man pluck them out of my hand." Let's look at these words: eternal life; never perish.

Christ doesn't offer a temporary solution. Eternal life is forever. "Never perish" means it is never going to happen. If you *truly* believe, as evidenced by a mighty change, then you have eternal life. And that means you will never perish.

You are, then, in the family of God, and no amount of extra revelation, no new scriptures, nothing can add to or take away from this promise. God cannot lie. Forever is forever and never perish means you never will. Praise God!

The way is just too simple for many. Sadly, the wise, the strong, the prideful, and those who cling to feel-good lies rather than truth will not receive it. When some are told that all they have to do is look to Jesus (for instance, as represented by the Israelites looking at a brass serpent on a pole to be saved from death from a poisonous bite), the way is just too simple for their minds. They retort, "What do you mean, all I have to do is look to Jesus to be saved? What about good works? Why, that's just 'cheap grace' that you're preaching now." But the Bible addresses this attitude, too. First Corinthians 1:18 declares that "the preaching of the cross is to them that perish foolishness; but unto us which are saved it is the power of God."

Please, friend, don't let the simplicity of the salvation of Christ keep you out of eternal life. It really is this simple: "And as

Moses lifted up the serpent in the wilderness, even so must the Son of man be lifted up: That whosoever believeth in him should not perish, but have eternal life" (John 3:14–15).

Jesus saves us from the poison of sin. He did this by taking that sin and nailing it to a cross so that whosoever looks to Him for salvation from the bite of sin and death will be saved.

## What the Bible teaches about heaven and what it means to be saved in it.

The Mormons are taught that salvation is only the beginning; but what does the Bible teach? As stated in earlier chapters, the Bible teaches that God the Father, Jesus Christ, and the Holy Spirit are one triune being. Jesus, who figuratively "sits on the right hand of the Father" is God. To say that there will be three different heavens one where Christ can go to and another that only the Spirit can go to, is to misunderstand the nature of God altogether. Remember, Jesus is on the throne of His Father. In Him dwells all the fullness of the Godhead. If you are with Christ, you are also with the Father. All believers of Christ are going to be with Him in a dwelling He has prepared for us, as Jesus said: "In my Father's house are many mansions: if it were not so, I would have told you. I go to prepare a place for you. And if I go and prepare a place for you, I will come again, and receive you unto myself; that where I am, there ye may be also" (John 14:2–3).

What are we being saved from? Salvation in its entirety is this: First, because of the death and resurrection of Christ, all mankind is saved from the curse of physical death that was a result of the sin of Adam. (The Mormons are correct in this.) All that have ever lived will stand before God in their flesh: "And though after my skin worms destroy this body, yet in my flesh shall I see God" (Job 19:26).

The second aspect of salvation is that you are being saved from the spiritual aspect of the same curse of Adam's sin— eternal separation from God and the fires of hell. This is called the second death. We must understand that we are all murderers, whoremongers, idolaters, and so on, as stated in Revelation 21:8: "But the fearful, and unbelieving, and the abominable, and murderers, and whoremongers, and sorcerers, and idolaters, and all liars, shall have their part in the lake which burneth with fire and brimstone: which is the second death."

You may say, "I've never killed; I've never stolen," and so forth. Yet the Bible says if you are guilty of breaking just one part of the Law, just one commandment, you are guilty of breaking the whole Law. "For whosoever shall keep the whole law, and yet offend in one point, he is guilty of all. For he that said, Do not commit adultery, said also, Do not kill. Now if thou commit no adultery, yet if thou kill, thou art become a transgressor of the law" (James 2:10–11).

This makes it so that no flesh can be justified before God. This means that no matter how good of a person we have been, if we have ever done just one small thing wrong, we are guilty of all. Who shall be saved then? "But Jesus beheld them, and said unto them, With men this is impossible; but with God all things are possible" (Matthew 19:26).

This is why we all need saving. It is impossible to be saved by our actions or works, even "after all we can do." But with God, all things are possible.

# Chapter 9

## The Fourth Article of Faith of the Church of Jesus Christ of Latter-day Saints

*Article 4. We believe that the first principles and ordinances of the Gospel are: first, Faith in the Lord Jesus Christ; second, Repentance; third, Baptism by immersion for the remission of sins; fourth, Laying on of hands for the gift of the Holy Ghost.*

## What This Statement Means from a Mormon Perspective

Mormons are taught to believe that salvation begins with Jesus. As discussed earlier, they are taught that the only way to access salvation is to turn from all your sin before you come to Him. Once a person does this, they must be baptized as a member of the Mormon church. They are taught that this baptism is what remits sin. Unless one is baptized in the way they prescribe and by those who have the express authority of God (by those who have had a direct succession of the laying on of the hands from Joseph Smith), one will not be able to go to heaven at all.

In the same understanding, they are taught that a person must also have this direct succession of the laying on of the hands in order to receive the Holy Ghost. They believe that only the apostles of Christ had the authority to act in the name of Christ, and that only they could "seal and bind" the things of God, and on His behalf, both in heaven and on earth.

This they teach, despite the fact that Christ Himself did not keep others who were not apostles from taking authority to use His name. (See Mark 9:38–39.)

Mormons believe that Christ gave the apostles the binding and sealing authority recorded in Matthew 16:18–19: "And I say also unto thee, That thou art Peter, and upon this rock I will build my church; and the gates of hell shall not prevail against it. And I will give unto thee the keys of the kingdom of heaven: and whatsoever thou shalt bind on earth shall be bound in heaven: and whatsoever thou shalt loose on earth shall be loosed in heaven."

They believe that only the apostles were given the right to act in the name of or on behalf of Jesus or the Father. This concept is similar to that of the Catholic church in that only the Popes have the direct succession of the apostles and are, therefore, the only ones with the right to act in the name of God.

This is also the same verse Mormons use to suggest that if a marriage is performed by someone with this binding and sealing authority it is also bound in heaven; therefore, the marriage will last for "time and eternity," as they often say.

**This concept of "eternal marriage" is a major draw to the church and is (at least, in practice and among family) used to keep members in the church.**

"Don't you want to be with us forever?" I have heard this phrase repeated many times to me by my loving, well-meaning family, and I'm sure that anyone who has dared to question the faith they once embraced as the only true church has heard it as well.

The church used to show outreach skits to temple visitors in Salt Lake City, Utah. In these commercials, a family is depicted as if they are deceased and now in heaven. Father and mother hold hands along with the children from tallest to youngest. Little tiny Tim is the smallest and still in diapers. "Families can be together forever" is the slogan, as if the children will forever be in a state of childhood. They do not present this as a doctrine that children will forever be small; I only mention it to expose the thinking behind this ideology—the thinking that the family unit will be segregated. The Bible teaches that we are all going to be one. All those who receive the "good news" about Jesus will be in the same family, a nation of kings and priests, a holy bride unto Christ. We will be married to Christ, not each other.

## What the Bible teaches about the principles of the gospel; Jesus as first and last.

In Revelation 1:17, we learn that Jesus is not only the first principle of the gospel, He is the first and the last: "And when I saw him, I fell at his feet as dead. And he laid his right hand upon me, saying unto me, Fear not; I am the first and the last." He is not only the beginning of salvation, or the "first principle of the gospel," but the whole of it. Jesus is the end result of our faith. First Peter 1:9 says, "Receiving the end of your faith, even the salvation of your souls." The end result is the complete salvation of our souls from death and hell.

The work of God is complete in Jesus Christ. All who accept Jesus as Lord are saved. Those who are saved will receive everything God has to offer—not part, not some, but all that God has will be ours to share in His kingdom. Consider these statements:

**Romans 8:32:** He that spared not his own Son, but delivered him up for us all, how shall he not with him also freely give us all things?

**1 Corinthians 3:21–23:** Therefore let no man glory in men. For all things are yours; whether Paul, or Apollos, or Cephas, or the world, or life, or death, or things present, or things to come; all are yours; and ye are Christ's; and Christ is God's.

I submit that not only will all believers enjoy all that God has to offer in heaven, but, just as a child of the king who stands to inherit the kingdom when he is old enough to receive it, in essence, that child already does own it all but simply must wait for the appointed time. We, too, already possess all that God has for us, right now. This is because the knowledge of the redemption of Christ and its acceptance qualifies us as "joint heirs with Christ." When we accept Jesus as our Savior, we truly begin to walk in eternity from that day forward. Everything Christ will receive, we also inherit with Him. "According as his divine power hath given unto us all things that pertain unto life and godliness, through the knowledge of him that hath called us to glory and virtue" (2 Peter 1:3). "He that overcometh shall inherit all things; and I will be his God, and he shall be my son" (Revelation 21:7).

The way Mormons have been taught leads them to feel that all that we do here is a precursor to what we will do in heaven. This mindset glorifies everything earthly and turns our actions here on earth into the actions of heaven. The Bible, however, teaches us that all the worldly things will be done away with. Mormons are taught that if procreation is good here on earth, it will be even better in heaven. If marriage to a wonderful spouse is pleasant here on earth, it will be even better in heaven. If raising children is wonderful, then more will be given in the age to come. This idea is taken to the extreme, in that if we can enjoy power here on earth, then we can become all powerful gods in heaven.

However the Bible tells us all these things are fleeting and will be changed into something much better. Things in Heaven are no more like earth than a seed looks like the wheat it produces. "And that which thou sowest, thou sowest not that body that shall be, but bare grain, it may chance of wheat, or of some other grain" (1 Corinthians 15:37).

The bodies we have in heaven are not going to be like what we have now any more than a grain of wheat looks like the plant that comes from it. "Who shall change our vile body, that it may be fashioned like unto his glorious body, according to the working whereby he is able even to subdue all things unto himself" (Philippians 3:21).

We will not be concerned with the things of earth. In heaven, we will not be married nor get married; we will not be as male or females are here on earth. We will all be as one in Christ. We, the church, will be married to Christ. "For in the resurrection they neither marry, nor are given in marriage, but are as the angels of God in heaven" (Matthew 22:30). "There is neither Jew nor Greek, there is neither bond nor free, there is neither male nor female: for ye are all one in Christ Jesus" (Galatians 3:28).

Everything of this earth will pass away, we aren't given a complete picture of what it will be like. "But as it is written, Eye hath not seen, nor ear heard, neither have entered into the heart of man, the things which God hath prepared for them that love him" (1 Corinthians 2:9).

God has not revealed to mankind what He has in store for us in the kingdom of heaven. He has made it clear, however, that it will not be like this world. He has also made it clear, not only that family units won't be the same, but that all believers will be together in the same heavenly family known both as the bride of Christ and simply the children of God. Therefore, of course we will all be together forever in heaven. Families will be together forever—that is, all in that family who receive the Lord's salvation according to the revealed Word of God, the Bible.

We will all be as the angels of God living in peace and common love for each other. Free of the impurities of life that come from the systems of this world. Can you imagine? Not only will we not be bound by earthly marriages, we will be free to enjoy each other's company in all purity and without the restrictions of time; all of us in perfect love and unity. No jealousies, no limitation on sharing the purest of love for each other. A love stronger than that between a man and a woman, for each person in Heaven. A kingdom of best friends, a nation of lovers in the purest sense.

King David gave us a small picture of this kind of love as recorded in 2 Samuel 1:26: "I am distressed for thee, my brother Jonathan: very pleasant hast thou been unto me: thy love to me was wonderful, passing the love of women." This is, of course, not some sick perversion of homosexuality, but of pure brotherly love, heavenly love after the heart of God.

## What the Bible teaches about baptism.

The word *baptism* is rightly understood by the Mormon church to mean the complete immersion of a body in water. The literal Greek meaning of the word is to dip something into dye, permanently staining it. In other words, we are completely dyed in the blood of Christ. When something is dyed, you can no longer see the color it once was. In this sense, when God looks at us, He no longer sees us and our sin, but the blood of Christ. We are then pronounced just and holy, unable to be convicted of sin—unblameable. Consider this passage from Colossians 1:21–23:

"And you, that were sometime alienated and enemies in your mind by wicked works, yet now hath he reconciled in the body of his flesh through death, to present you holy and unblameable and unreproveable in his sight: If ye continue in the faith grounded and settled, and be not moved away from the hope of the gospel, which ye have heard, and which was preached to every creature which is under heaven; where of I Paul am made a minister."

Baptism is the outward sign of what God has done on the inside. It is your public commitment that you desire to "continue in the faith…and be not moved." However, if it were a "saving ordinance," there would have been no need to have been baptized more than once, as some of the followers of John were:

"And it came to pass, that, while Apollos was at Corinth, Paul having passed through the upper coasts came to Ephesus: and finding certain disciples, he said unto them, Have ye received the Holy Ghost since ye believed? And they said unto him, We have not so much as heard whether there be any Holy Ghost.

And he said unto them, Unto what then were ye baptized? And they said, Unto John's baptism. Then said Paul, John verily baptized with the baptism of repentance, saying unto the people, that they should believe on him which should come after him, that is, on Christ Jesus. When they heard that, they were baptized in the name of the Lord Jesus." (Acts 19:1–5)

Again, if baptism were a saving ordinance, the Mormons are being baptized "unto repentance," which was John's baptism. In theory, then, the Mormon's baptism is not unto Christ because He had a better baptism than the "baptism of repentance." Paul would have found no need to baptize them again if salvation came by "baptism for the remission of sins"—they would have already been washed.

Furthermore, if John had restored the ordinance of the baptism by personally giving that authority to Joseph Smith, then truly, that baptism of John (the baptism of repentance) was proven to be inadequate by Paul and replaced by a better baptism, not only unto repentance but unto Christ and His finished work alone.

This is the sum of the matter: baptism is an outward commitment to be fully washed, or dyed, unto something. John's followers committed to follow John into repentance in preparation for the coming of the Lord. They publicly committed to follow John unto Christ's coming. The followers of Christ were baptized to show their commitment to Christ and be completely changed by His doctrine (fully dyed). This repentance however, was not simply outward, but inward. This baptism "unto Christ" brought salvation—not for the act, but for the faith that brought the act.

## The man on the cross next to Jesus, and what he teaches us.

When the man crucified next to Christ asked that Jesus to remember him when He got to His kingdom, Christ replied, "To day shalt thou be with me in paradise" (Luke 23:43). I know, I know—the Mormons teach that this is because the righteous go to spirit paradise while awaiting the resurrection. This, however, is neither consistent with the Bible nor their own teachings.

On the website, www.LDS.org, the following is posted:

"**Baptism for the Dead.** Thus, those who die without a knowledge of Christ have the opportunity to hear the glad message of redemption, exercise faith, and repent of their sins. But what of baptism? As the Lord taught Nicodemus, a person must be baptized—born of water—before he can enter the kingdom of heaven (John 3:5). Jesus himself was baptized "to fulfill all righteousness" (Matt. 3:15), and he instructed his apostles to baptize those who accepted the gospel message, telling them "He that believeth and is baptized shall be saved" (Mark 16:16). How, then, can those who died without the chance to be baptized receive this ordinance? The answer is that they can receive it vicariously. Just as Jesus performed a labor for us that we could not perform for ourselves, so can we perform the ordinance of baptism for those who have died, allowing them the opportunity to become heirs of salvation."

According to this, as well as other Mormon doctrine, the man next to Jesus would not have gone to spirit paradise "to day." According to their teaching, he would first have had to be preached to, understand the gospel, and then be baptized by someone standing in proxy for him. According to their teaching, this man would have been in spirit prison because of his sinful life until someone could receive the ordinance of baptism for him on earth.

This, of course, would have been impossible to happen "to day." The man had no time to be taught the gospel, to be baptized, to experience the laying on of the hands—none of the things the Mormons say must happen before one who is a sinner is released from spirit prison into paradise.

But remember, Christ Himself pronounced that the man next to Him on the cross would be in paradise with Him that very day. This is no small point, friend. These things cannot be rightly reconciled because they are not true. Baptism is not a saving ordinance—belief in Jesus Christ is. Anyone who believes in Christ and is completely covered in the blood (baptized/completely dyed) will be saved. The man on the cross next to Jesus— at the end of his life with no chance of works, no laying on of the hands, no chance to prove his repentance, no temple marriage, no water baptism—with nothing but his faith-filled plea, "remember me," received Christ as His Savior and was saved and accepted into the paradise of God. Just like all who receive Jesus on simple faith alone are saved and accepted (John 3:16).

But what of the place where Christ told Nicodemus that one must be "born of the water"? Doesn't that mean you must be baptized?

This is a great question. In order to understand this truth, you must first understand that not everything you have been taught as a Mormon is truth. All scripture must be reconciled with scripture. God cannot lie, and His Word is truth and free of contradiction. Therefore, it is important to understand that being "born of the water" is not to be baptized.

This Mormon concept may sound very logical because of the way it has been presented—just as many other teachings sound logical in man's wisdom, but simply do not line up with the Word of God. There is a great danger when a verse is made into a doctrine of itself, rather than allowing the Word to clarify itself as a whole. When, for example, the Bible says "By grace are ye saved," other verses must be weighed out and balanced by that truth. On the other hand, when we read "faith without works is dead," we must allow the Spirit of God to reconcile the two through the Word, rather than assume that there is a flaw in the text or a contradiction.

We must be humble enough to realize that if there is a contradiction or flaw, it is in our understanding, not in the Word of God. I'm sure you, too, have heard people twist the Word of God in order to connect the dots, so to speak. They are able, at least in their own minds, to make the Word say just about anything they wish. If these deceptions are repeated many times, they begin to sound familiar. Once they are familiar, they are then perceived as truth by those who do not understand and are unwilling to question what they are told.

## So what is being "born of the water"?

This teaching was taken from a recorded conversation between Christ and a man named Nicodemus. Anyone who has read the Bible or been to church knows this conversation well, as it contains many truths vital to the salvation of mankind. The flawed premise today is that being "born of the water" is baptism. The truth is, rather, that Christ was talking about the rebirth, the spiritual birth that happens when you are born from above and renewed by the "washing of the water of the Word." Remember, Nicodemus had just asked Jesus how one could be born again when he is old. Answering this very question, Christ began at Nicodemus's thinking of natural birth (of water) and expanded it to include the spiritual rebirth.

We are all first "born of the water" in our mother's womb, as Nicodemus inferred. All are not "born from above," however. If you must spiritualize this, then when we are born again, we are born first of the "water of the Word" (it is the "truth [of God's Word that] sets us free"), and then of the Spirit. John 4:14 says, "But whosoever drinketh of the water that I shall give him shall never thirst; but the water that I shall give him shall be in him a well of water springing up into everlasting life." Ephesians 5:26 says Christ gave himself for the church "that he might sanctify and cleanse it with the washing of water by the word."

The Word of God is the means by which God cleanses us. We are "clean by the word I have spoken," says the Lord. Indeed, all believers are baptized with Christ, crucified with Him, and raised with Him. When Christ was baptized, it "fulfilled all righteousness" for those who die in Him without this ordinance (such as the man next to Him on the cross). Babies who die would fall into this same category. Whatever it is, it's more merciful than we are thinking.

Please understand, this is not intended to say that we shouldn't baptize in water. Every believer should be baptized, as this is a symbol of the rebirth that has taken place inwardly. It is a public commitment to die to your old self and live unto Christ. Spiritually speaking, however, when we receive Christ, we accept His baptism as our own, His death on our behalf, and we are raised with Him from death because of His resurrection. He "fulfilled all righteousness" vicariously for all who receive Him. Everything we needed to do except receive Him, He did for us. He is our "saving ordinances."

## This life is the time to accept the Lord, not the hereafter.

Although this is a bit off topic, we touched on the afterlife and the Mormon teaching that vicarious work would be performed there for the dead. I want to shed some clarity on this subject before we move on.

This life is the time when we must come to Christ. After this life, we have nothing to look forward to if we are sinners, but the judgment. There is no second chance. "It is appointed unto men once to die, but after this the judgment" (Hebrews 9:27).

We only live once—even the world likes to say that—but the Bible says after that comes the judgment. Therefore, this life is the only time we have to come to the Lord. "For he saith, I have heard thee in a time accepted, and in the day of salvation have I succoured thee: behold, now is the accepted time; behold, now is the day of salvation" (Hebrews 9:27).

In the grave—in death—there is no teaching of the Lord; none of His wonderful ways will be declared. In addition, there will be no chance to pass from heaven to hell nor from hell to heaven after we die.

**Psalm 88:10–11:** Wilt thou shew wonders to the dead? shall the dead arise and praise thee? Selah. Shall thy lovingkindness be declared in the grave? or thy faithfulness in destruction?

**Luke 16:26:** And beside all this, between us and you there is a great gulf fixed: so that they which would pass from hence to you cannot; neither can they pass to us, that would come from thence.

## No sin is held against God's elect, we are completely free of all guilt.

**Romans 8:33–34:** Who shall lay any thing to the charge of God's elect? It is God that justifieth. Who is he that condemneth? It is Christ that died, yea rather, that is risen again, who is even at the right hand of God, who also maketh intercession for us.

Nothing can be "laid to our charge," because Christ paid for everything we've done, everything we will do. However, this is only true for those who truly are His "elect." You must endure to the end to be saved. Only His true followers will even be able to endure until the end. Rest assured, if you don't know Him, if you are not His, you will not be able to stand on your own, nor "endure till the end." Only those who truly believe that God raised Jesus from the dead, to the point that this belief produces the fruits of right living and a commitment to live for Christ, will endure till the end. Only these will be saved. Matthew 24:12–13 says: "And because iniquity shall abound, the love of many shall wax cold. But he that shall endure unto the end, the same shall be saved."

Consider Matthew 13:4–8:

And when he sowed, some seeds fell by the way side, and the fowls came and devoured them up: Some fell upon stony places, where they had not much earth: and forthwith they sprung up, because they had no deepness of earth: and when the sun was up, they were scorched; and because they had no root, they withered away. And some fell among thorns; and the thorns sprung up, and choked them. But other fell into good ground, and brought forth fruit, some an hundredfold, some sixtyfold, some thirtyfold.

Many will hear the words of God and know that they are true. Many will begin to walk in this direction, and faith will begin to sprout, but only the seed of God that was planted in "good ground," the ground of faith, will bring forth fruit.

## What the Bible teaches about receiving of the gift of the Holy Ghost.

Let me start by pointing out that there are many times in the Bible that the Holy Ghost was given by the apostles' "laying on of the hands." When the day of Pentecost came, the Holy Ghost was given from God to the people without the laying on of the hands. While there is evidence that this type of transference did take place, it was not exclusive.

For instance, in Acts 10:44, "While Peter yet spake these words, the Holy Ghost fell on all them which heard the word." In this case, Peter only spoke, and the Holy Ghost fell on them that heard. There is an important issue raised about this topic—the issue of authority—which we will address in the next chapter.

# Chapter 10

## The Fifth and Sixth Articles of Faith of the Church of Jesus Christ of Latter-day Saints

*Article 5. We believe that a man must be called of God, by prophecy, and by the laying on of hands by those who are in authority, to preach the Gospel and administer in the ordinances thereof.*

*Article 6. We believe in the same organization that existed in the Primitive Church, namely, apostles, prophets, pastors, teachers, evangelists, and so forth.*

We will address these two articles together over the next two chapters because the concepts overlap. Every Christian may recite these same two articles, if not for the meaning behind them in a Mormon perspective.

One must indeed be called by God to administer the things of God. What is meant by this statement in a Mormon mind-set, however, is that only those in direct priesthood succession from Joseph Smith have the right to administer in the things of the gospel. Joseph claimed to get his priesthood directly from Peter, James, and John in a physical visitation from the three. He claimed the three appeared to him and laid hands on him for the transference of the "Melchizedek priesthood." This, Joseph claimed, put himself in direct succession to the original apostles.

With this transference, Joseph was the only authorized representative on earth with the authority to restore the gospel to its original state when Christ set up the church with the original twelve apostles. Joseph claimed he could then set up "the only true church on earth with the keys of the priesthood."

Joseph also claimed that God had given him revelation as to how to set up the church in accordance with the original church of God, with a prophet acting in the name of Jesus Christ, then twelve apostles, high priests, bishops, teachers, and deacons.

## The general makeup of the leadership of the Mormon church. (This is not an all inclusive list.)

The Mormon church is one of the most well-organized churches I ever seen. There is a leader in every situation. The style of leadership is fashioned with a down-line delegation of authority such as Moses set up. There is a leader over anything from two individuals to worldwide leaders over millions. A general breakdown of their leadership offices from least to greatest is as follows:

Deacons are around twelve years old, teachers around fourteen, priests around sixteen. These are said to be offices of the "Aaronic" priesthood, which also includes the office of bishop. The office of bishop is similar to what Christians call a pastor. Joseph claimed to have received this Aaronic priesthood power from the resurrected John the Baptist of the Bible.

Around the age of nineteen or twenty, the young men are ordained as elders. The elders hold the Melchizedek priesthood. Elders are the ones you see on bikes in twos, serving as missionaries. The Melchizedek priesthood includes the offices of elder, high priest, seventy, patriarch, apostle, and president of the church.

Women do not possess the priesthood in the Mormon faith, nor do they hold any congregational leadership roles. Woman do have leadership roles as Sunday school teachers, Sunday school presidents, and leaders of women's groups such as the Relief Society. Each of these offices is overseen by a male.

All positions in the church, including the office of bishop, are on a volunteer basis only. The members, including myself when I was one, take great pride in this fact, because they feel that anyone not receiving compensation for doing the work of God must be a true servant of God.

The church is led worldwide by the president of the church, known to them as the "modern day prophet."

The prophet serves as Moses did in the place of God on earth. They serve for life and are usually called from the senior members of the quorum of the twelve apostles or the first counselor (one of two counselors) to the president of the church, also known as the prophet.

Normally, the first counselor is chosen to succeed the presidency upon the death of the leader. The office can also be filled by the ranking or senior member of the quorum of the twelve apostles, known in the church as "the Twelve." Under the Twelve are the general leadership of the church, comprised of "the quorum of seventies," which are seventy elders who serve in the church, usually individually overseeing a whole region or country. Being a member of the quorum of the seventies does not mean that there are exactly seventy in number, however, as it is more of an office than an exact number of elders. They use Luke 10:1 for this ideology: "After these things the Lord appointed other seventy also, and sent them two and two before his face into every city and place, whither he himself would come."

As stated earlier, this is only a general outline, as there are many positions throughout the church from a congregational or local church known as a "ward." Several wards make up a "stake." Several stakes make up an "area." Several areas make up a "region." Each level has a leader of its own who answers to a higher leader above him. A few brief examples of leadership names are "stake president;" "area president," and so on. Usually a member of the seventy oversees a region.

None of these offices can be aspired to—instead, the current leadership over that office calls someone, through the purported gift of prophecy, to fill positions.

## What the Bible teaches about church leadership, the priesthood, and the authority to act in the name of God.

When God set up the church under Moses, He originally asked only Moses to lead the people out of bondage. Moses felt that because he was "slow of speech," he was not a good spokesperson for God. God therefore began, from that time forward, to set up a leadership delegation. He commanded that Aaron would be set as a prophet, and Moses would be in the place of God to Aaron and the people. "And he shall be thy spokesman unto the people: and he shall be, even he shall be to thee instead of a mouth, and thou shalt be to him instead of God" (Exodus 4:16).

God's desire was to commune with His chosen people face to face. However, the people rejected this offer and told God to speak to Moses, and they would do what Moses said on God's behalf. "And all the people saw the thunderings, and the lightnings, and the noise of the trumpet, and the mountain smoking: and when the people saw it, they removed, and stood afar off. And they said unto Moses, Speak thou with us, and we will hear: but let not God speak with us, lest we die" (Exodus 20:18–19).

In the process of time, the burden became too great for Moses to judge all of Israel. So, on the advice of his father-in-law, he set up lower judges naming "captains of tens, fifties, hundreds and thousands" over the people.

Later, as the children of Israel occupied the promised land, they again rejected God as their leader and asked for a king. This grieved God, but He consented and set up a new system. The new system had the effect of pushing God even farther from the individual. The highest leadership now consisted of prophet, high priest and king.

From this time forward, the duties of the kingdom were split up between the spiritual, the matters of state, and all civic duties (such as military duties, public welfare, and such).

The role of the prophet was to stand in the place of God for the people, to inquire God's will, and to give these messages from God to the people. These messages were known as prophecies.

The role of the priest was to minister to the Lord on behalf of the people in matters of the temple. Work consisted of offering sacrifices to God, first for themselves, then on behalf of the people. These sacrifices were designed to temporarily cover sin in order to gain forgiveness and access to the Lord and His favor and blessings. Once each year, the high priest would enter the "Holy of Holies," where the presence of the Lord resided, to make intercession and offer the atoning sacrifice for the people.

The whole purpose of the temple was to house the presence of the Lord. The whole purpose of the ordinances performed there was to cleanse the people in order to gain access to the presence of the Lord. This is solely because they had rejected a face-to-face relationship with Him. Nothing else was designed to go on there.

This temple was designed by God as a "type and a shadow" (a representation) of the heavenly dwelling of God, not made with hands. Nothing was hidden, but rather, everything was clearly and specifically laid out. We will discuss this in more detail shortly on the topic of the Temple.

## The leadership of the church in Christ's time.

It is easy to see, from a biblical standpoint, that by the time Christ came into the world, the leadership of the church had been severely compromised. From a historical standpoint as well, the Romans had assumed domination over the land of Israel and no prophets had been leading the church for about four hundred years.

According to the historian Josephus (AD 37–100), Jason, the brother of the current high priest at the time of Antiochus IV, offered a large sum of money in order to be appointed as high priest. It is clear to most, and a commonly held belief among all Christian sects, that the system of leadership was fragmented and uninspired by the time of Christ's birth. So uninspired and blind to the leading of the Spirit of the Lord were they, that they had the very Son of God crucified.

## How does Christ fit into the leadership of the church in relation to Moses?

The leaders of the people of Israel at the time of Christ had unwittingly fulfilled the scriptures in the worst possible way. Blindly, they rejected and killed their own Messiah. The very Messiah they had been waiting for, singing about, and praying about for hundreds of years, they crucified.

Even though the leadership of the day "sat in Moses's seat," according to the words of Christ, they no longer were sanctioned individually by Christ. While He did still honor their position, He gave no reverence to the persons who filled them (Matthew 23:2).

When Christ was crucified, He fulfilled all the requirements of the Law as the perfect sacrifice for sin. Whereas the high priest used to have to enter the Holy of Holies for the people, Christ, the great High Priest, entered in but once and "sat down on the right hand of the Father."

Whereas there used to be a separation between God and man—the veil of the temple separating the Holy of Holies from the outer courts—this separation, as a symbol of Christ becoming the mediator between God and man, was torn from top to bottom, thus giving mankind full access to the Father, no other mediation required. Several passages attest to this fact.

**Mark 15:38:** And the veil of the temple was rent in twain from the top to the bottom.

**Hebrews 9:12:** Neither by the blood of goats and calves, but by his own blood he entered in once into the holy place, having obtained eternal redemption for us.

**Hebrews 10:10–17:** By the which will we are sanctified through the offering of the body of Jesus Christ once for all. And every priest standeth daily ministering and offering often-times the same sacrifices, which can never take away sins: But this man, after he had offered one sacrifice for sins for ever, sat down on the right hand of God; from henceforth expecting till his enemies be made his footstool. For by one offering he hath perfected for ever them that are sanctified. Whereof the Holy Ghost also is a witness to us: for after that he had said before, This is the covenant that I will make with them after those days, saith the Lord, I will put my laws into their hearts, and in their minds will I write them; And their sins and iniquities will I remember no more.

Thus, the intercessory position of high priest became obsolete for all humans to fill because it was now perpetually filled by the one who has eternal life and therefore will never need to be replaced.

## The order of Melchizedek.

**Hebrews 5:4–6:** And no man taketh this honour unto himself, but he that is called of God, as was Aaron. So also Christ glorified not himself to be made an high priest; but he that said unto him, Thou art my Son, to day have I begotten thee. As he saith also in another place, Thou art a priest for ever after the order of Melchizedek.

The Mormons feel that no one can receive or aspire to the offices of the priesthood without direct secession (though laying on of the hands) from one called of God. This person must also have been ordained in the same manner by one who already has had this authority conferred upon them.

While this was true in the days of the high priests, Christ made all believers "a nation of kings and priests." In the days of the Law or the "Old Covenant," it was only a matter of family lineage. Not just anyone could take this honor—they must be from the chosen family to serve.

Again, however, this is no longer in effect. We serve under and in the authority of the great High Priest, called by an oath of God rather than by the promise of a priesthood lineage alone. This first priesthood honor was granted by inheritance, not by an oath. Therefore, Jesus did not take the honor of being the High Priest unto Himself, but was ordained by God. Hebrews 7:17 says, "For he testifieth, Thou art a priest for ever after the order of Melchizedek." Jesus was the only other person called after the order of Melchizedek.

Remember, only one high priest was ordained, and this was for life. All lesser priesthood holders were not called by God, except Aaron and the children of Levi. After Aaron's calling, his children and the children of Levi served in suggestion by families, father to sons. The high priests were taken from Aaron's lineage, not after the order of Melchizedek as the Mormons teach.

## Done away in Christ

All high priests served for life. Jesus, who has an unending life, now abides forever as High Priest. So there could be none to follow, because He entered in "once" then sat down at the right hand of the Father. The job was done, and the veil that separated God from the people was no longer needed.

From that day forward, there was no longer a need for a new high priest to take Christ's place. From this day forward, we serve under the express authority of Christ alone. Truly, all believers are now called and commissioned for the work and have full access to all the rights, powers, and privileges of the high priest. We no longer have anything, or anyone, standing between us and the face of God. It is now only a matter of our faith in Christ alone and our willingness to receive His free gift. We truly have full access to God and all that He has to offer. Christ alone is our authority to act in the name of God. Truly, we do not take this honor unto ourselves, but rather, it is a gift of God in Christ and given by His Word spoken through the holy apostles.

## What about prophets to lead the whole church?

Hebrews 8:11 says, "And they shall not teach every man his neighbour, and every man his brother, saying, Know the Lord: for all shall know me, from the least to the greatest." Before the day of Pentecost, the Holy Spirit was found among men at times, but God stood, as it were, in the outer courts of them because they were unclean and God can not dwell in an unclean Temple. From Pentecost forward, men were given the gift of the Holy Ghost and were pronounced clean through the Word spoken, wherein the Lord moved His dwelling from an earthly sanctuary made with hands to a temple not constructed by man but made in His very image. Thus the Holy of Holies is now found deep within each justified person's heart.

This new indwelling of the Spirit fulfilled this scripture found in Joel 2:28–29: "And it shall come to pass afterward, that I will pour out my spirit upon all flesh; and your sons and your daughters shall prophesy, your old men shall dream dreams, your young men shall see visions: And also upon the servants and upon the handmaids in those days will I pour out my spirit."

Here we see that no longer would only great and mighty oracles of God carry His presence and have access to His power, but even the lowest in society—the servants—would prophesy. Children and old men, young women as well, were now able to receive and speak the Word of the Lord for themselves. No one any longer needs to ask (though many of us do because of unbelief), "what does the Lord say about this or that?" Now that the Spirit dwells within us, each believer is given the Holy Ghost as a prophetic guide and "alongside helper."

## Christ as Prophet, Priest, and King.

The role of the central prophet was no longer needed after Christ's triumph; Christ forever stands as the ultimate Prophet of the church. In addition, the whole church body became a nation of prophets, priests, and kings along with Christ. This is known as the "priesthood authority of the believer." This is our claim to act in His name, His Word.

From Christ's advent forward, the leadership changed. We no longer needed a human to fill the role of prophet, to sit in Moses's seat. We no longer needed a new high priest, nor a new king, as Jesus fulfills all three and will never leave His post. In Him, we no longer need to follow our fellow mankind in the things of God, as we who are in Christ became a nation of prophets, priests, and kings, a royal priesthood after the order of the Son of God. He "hath made us kings and priests unto God and his Father; to him be glory and dominion for ever and ever" (Revelation 1:6).

In Matthew 20:25–28, Christ gave us a picture of the modern leadership that He desired for his church.

But Jesus called them unto him, and said, Ye know that the princes of the Gentiles exercise dominion over them, and they that are great exercise authority upon them. But it shall not be so among you: but whosoever will be great among you, let him be your minister; and whosoever will be chief among you, let him be your servant: Even as the Son of man came not to be ministered unto, but to minister, and to give his life a ransom for many.

In summary, Christ doesn't call prophet leaders as Moses did, because He is all three and abides forever as such. Note, however, that there are many that prophesy as stated in Joel. These, while operating in this gift, are not in the role of Moses as the singular leader for the church at large. In our day, Christ is calling for servant leaders. No one therefore stands between us and God in authority. There is no down-line delegation of authority from overseers to helpers. Instead, we are all to be working side by side with Christ alone at the head.

## The church of God isn't an organization, it's a people.

The church of God is a people, it is in us and among us. "Neither shall they say, Lo here! or, lo there! for, behold, the kingdom of God is within you" (Luke 17:21). The Greek language here implies that not only is He within us, he is among us.

We the people of God are the church. This means there is no perfect church on the earth, because none of us is perfect. Organizationally speaking, this means there is no "only true church on the face of the earth" because no one in the church will have all the answers; nor are we given perfect revelation of the things of God. We don't need to look for perfect leaders or a perfect organization to follow, because we all serve a perfect leader in Christ.

Even when we do get prophecy, it is tainted and dim. It is only when Christ returns that we "shall know as we are known" of the Father. Until that time, the church is like Peter walking on the water. The only foundation for his feet was the faith he had in Christ to stand, not the organization or structure of the boat.

We the Christian church at large don't therefore stand on the "-ologies" of mankind. We stand on this faith alone. We are not required to know all the mysteries of God in order to be saved by them. We are required to have faith in Christ alone in order to be saved. Every other ordinance is a matter of sanctification, not justification.

Every leadership role of the church is merely an overseer's role to ensure that the weak are not devoured by the crafty and that sound doctrine is upheld. No, we do not all agree. Yes, there are those who are, or can be called Christian who have opposing views. These views never change the truth, however. True followers of Christ are not counted in the rolls of any one organization, but in the records of God.

God alone knows who the true believers are, regardless of what form of (true) Christianity he/she may cling to. I say "true" because, as Christ said, not everyone that says "Lord, Lord" is a

Christian. I will not attempt to show a list of churches I feel are in, and the ones that are out; but, I will show a biblical perspective that would help one make a wise choice among the many, truly Christian denominations.

# Chapter 11

## Continuation of the Fifth and Sixth Articles of Faith

*Article 5. We believe that a man must be called of God, by prophecy, and by the laying on of hands by those who are in authority, to preach the Gospel and administer in the ordinances thereof.*

*Article 6. We believe in the same organization that existed in the Primitive Church, namely, apostles, prophets, pastors, teachers, evangelists, and so forth.*

### Did the only true church die out with the apostles as the Mormons suggest?

The apostles had the task of setting forth the gospel to the world as special witnesses of Christ. Witnesses who had personally seen Him, and who had specific revelation for the raising up of the new covenant church of God. They were given the infallible revelation of the mystery of God in how that God would bring the gospel to the whole world, both Gentile and Jew.

Contrary to Mormon teachings found in The Pearl of Great Price and the Book of Mormon, the prophets of old were not given the full revelation that the Gentiles would also be equal with them. This is made clear in Ephesians 3:4–7:

"Whereby, when ye read, ye may understand my knowledge in the mystery of Christ which in other ages was not made known unto the sons of men, as it is now revealed unto his holy apostles and prophets by the Spirit; That the Gentiles should be fellow heirs, and of the same body, and partakers of his promise in Christ by the gospel: Whereof I was made a minister, according to the gift of the grace of God given unto me by the effectual working of his power."

Many of the writings of Joseph Smith that are held as scripture teach that the prophets of these writings had a revelation of the preaching of the gospel to the gentiles. For instance, 1 Nephi 13:42 says,

"And the time cometh that he shall manifest himself unto all nations, both unto the Jews and also unto the Gentiles; and after he has manifested himself unto the Jews and also unto the Gentiles, then he shall manifest himself unto the Gentiles and also unto the Jews, and the last shall be first, and the first shall be last."

The people of God and the prophets of old had the revelation that God would be a light to the Gentiles; they where not however, given the revelation to the degree that Joseph's writings suggest.

There are many teachings on this subject from a Mormon perspective, but the Bible proves this a false concept. Before Peter was given the first revelation about how God would also bring the Gentiles into salvation through faith, this was a foreign concept to the Jewish nation. Later, Paul, who also became the apostle to the Gentiles, was given the full revelation for the reconciliation of the Gentiles to God. Before this time, it was revealed that the Gentiles would one day praise Him, that the root of Jesse would be a light, but the full revelation didn't come until Paul's ministry.

## The catholic church is not the same as the Catholic church.

Before the days of the Catholic church at Rome with the Pope and the church fathers and such, there was an area of church history in which the catholic church—the word *catholic* means "church at large"—was the only Christian church. It is obvious to most Christian believers that when the institutionalized Catholic church came into power in Rome, it did not honor the word of God above that of the leadership of the church, known as the church fathers.

It is my great conviction that while the Catholic church may have strayed, the true catholic church, the church at large, did not. Throughout the centuries there have been many faithful, godly followers of Christ, some within this Mormon church, as well. I believe it is as in the days of Elijah who, after witnessing the murder of his fellow servants of God, thought that perhaps he was the only man of God left alive.

Unknown to Elijah was the fact that God had reserved to Himself those who had not turned away and bowed to Baal. Notice the text from Romans 11:3–4, where Paul reminds those around him of God's response to Elijah's plight: "Lord, they have killed thy prophets, and digged down thine altars; and I am left alone, and they seek my life. But what saith the answer of God unto him? I have reserved to myself seven thousand men, who have not bowed the knee to the image of Baal."

God has always reserved to Himself a remnant. While there was a "falling away" by the Catholic church (the one with the Pope), the church at large (the true followers of Christ) will and always have remained faithful, if only a few. Have mistakes been made? Yes.

Does this mean that faith in the work of Christ on the cross was no longer the only means by which we claim authority to act in God's name? Absolutely not—Christ is our only claim to priesthood authority. His work is not undone when we as the church stumble or make mistakes.

The "falling away" that was predicted before His return in 2 Thessalonians 2:3 was accomplished in the Catholic church. This passage reads: "Let no man deceive you by any means: for that day shall not come, except there come a falling away first, and that man of sin be revealed, the son of perdition."

We now are subject to receive revelation but no longer as Word of God scripture, because the gospel has been set forth, and the way clearly set.

## What about paid pastors? Doesn't that prove that men are doing it for money? What does the Bible say?

From the beginning of the building of the kingdom of God, the Lord has made prevision for the leadership of His people. When the Lord gave an inheritance to the people of God by families, He did not give an inheritance to those that served Him—their portion was the Lord. Read Numbers 18:23–24:

"But the Levites shall do the service of the tabernacle of the congregation, and they shall bear their iniquity: it shall be a statute for ever throughout your generations, that among the children of Israel they have no inheritance. But the tithes of the children of Israel, which they offer as an heave offering unto the LORD, I have given to the Levites to inherit: therefore I have said unto them, Among the children of Israel they shall have no inheritance."

While others could own property and prosper according to the labor of their own hands, the servants of God were to be blessed by the provision of the Lord only. In this way, their income was in direct proportion to the faithfulness of the people whom they served.

God not only set up a system for the leaders of the people, but for the singers and musicians, doormen and others. "And these are the singers, chief of the fathers of the Levites, who remaining in the chambers were free: for they were employed in that work day and night" (1 Chronicles 9:33).

Paul's assertion that he did not "charge" the church of Corinth, was by no means an indication that God no longer provided for His servants this way. What Paul was saying was that he did not allow this particular church the blessings of giving because of their own fear that Paul or others might have been doing the work of God for money. Paul was still provided for by other churches. "I robbed other churches, taking wages of them, to do you service" (2 Corinthians 11:8).

Again, Paul's argument was that the man of God does still have the same right to the inheritance of those who receive blessings at the hand of the man of God. 1 Corinthians 9:9–11 says,

"For it is written in the law of Moses, Thou shalt not muzzle the mouth of the ox that treadeth out the corn. Doth God take care for oxen? Or saith he it altogether for our sakes? For our sakes, no doubt, this is written: that he that ploweth should plow in hope; and that he that thresheth in hope should be partaker of his hope. If we have sown unto you spiritual things, is it a great thing if we shall reap your carnal things?"

Paul was not saying that this principle was being done away by any means; he was rather reaffirming its validity. Just because some have used this principle for the gain of "filthy lucre" does not make it an evil thing to use this God-ordained principle correctly, as Paul also did.

Many parents have abused their children; that does not make all parents abusers. Many men have cheated on their wives; that does not make all men cheaters. In the same way, many fakes have given the church a bad name because of their misuse of this God-ordained principle. Some have started out on the right track, only to have been led away by the same greed. This does not mean that everyone that is a minister in the things of God is after filthy lucre.

As pertaining to the Levitical family being the only ones in New Testament times who were worthy of receiving tithes, the ministers of Christ were not limited to the house of Levi—Paul, for instance, was of the tribe of Benjamin. They were priests after the order of Melchizedek in Christ, not after the order of Aaron. Philippians 3:5 describes Paul as being "circumcised the eighth day, of the stock of Israel, of the tribe of Benjamin, an Hebrew of the Hebrews; as touching the law, a Pharisee."

## Other uses of tithe monies.

In the purest form of the use of tithes, they were not originally given to be used to build buildings and pay the light bills. Tithes where strictly for the inheritance of the servants of God. These other items should be handled with offerings. Second Kings 12:16 says, "The trespass money and sin money was not brought into the house of the Lord: it was the priests'."

Many overseers (bishops) in the Mormon church choose to use the tithes to do all manner of upkeep of the church. This is not wrong, I believe, as it is theirs to do with as they please. I think it is the duty of the church body of believers however to maintain such things (in the purest of uses of this principle). We as the church often choose to have a building for the convenience. This building is not the church, however; it is where the church meets. This meeting place could be in any convenient place chosen.

## We are the temple of God.

We the people of God are the church or bride of Christ. We are also the temple of God. There is no more need for temples built by human hands—the Holy of Holies is now in the heart of every believer of Christ. "Know ye not that ye are the temple of God, and that the Spirit of God dwelleth in you?" (1 Corinthians 3:16).

Jesus made a temple without hands when He rose from the grave. "We heard him say, I will destroy this temple that is made with hands, and within three days I will build another made without hands" (Mark 14:58). His body is the veil that separates us from the throne of God. Any follower of Christ therefore does not need a temple made with hands to gain access to the Father. Jesus is our access forever. We that are in Him by faith are now the temple that houses the Holy Spirit of God. Our structural houses of worship may be honored as such, but only to the degree that they are set aside unto the Lord for holy use. They of themselves are not holy structures, as was the House of God. Even this house (the earthly sanctuary) was only a shadow of the real House made without hands. "Ye also, as lively stones, are built up a spiritual house, an holy priesthood, to offer up spiritual sacrifices, acceptable to God by Jesus Christ" (1 Peter 2:5).

## What does the church look like now?

**Ephesians 4:11–13:** And he gave some, apostles; and some, prophets; and some, evangelists; and some, pastors and teachers; For the perfecting of the saints, for the work of the ministry, for the edifying of the body of Christ: Till we all come in the unity of the faith, and of the knowledge of the Son of God, unto a perfect man, unto the measure of the stature of the fulness of Christ.

All of these gifts are in place to this day; the revelatory part of the apostles' work, however, was finished at the conclusion of their earthly ministry. We do not believe that there are now centralized apostles for the church at large, and we do not believe that the work of prophets or those that operate in these gifts are of the infallible nature of original apostles, whose job it was to set forth the kingdom in the last days.

The gospel was fully restored and the Bible completely set forth to the degree that salvation and the way to reconciliation of mankind is complete in the canon of scripture we call the Bible.

## The biblical leadership of the church.

The servant leaders of this age are to lead the kind of life of that of Paul who confidently instructed in 1 Corinthians 4:16: "Wherefore I beseech you, be ye followers of me." Although there have been those leaders whose lives do not warrant following, true servants of God can say this same phrase with confidence, even though no one is perfect. This phrase is best understood in this fashion: "In every area of my life that is an example of Christ-like living, do the same things." Each leader of today, regardless of their denomination, should be able to repeat this phrase. The word of God calls for leaders to be above reproach or blameless. "A bishop then must be blameless, the husband of one wife, vigi-lant, sober, of good behaviour, given to hospitality, apt to teach" (1 Timothy 3:2).

The Bible specifically teaches that the offices of deacon and elder in the church were not for young boys of twelve to nine-teen years of age as the Mormons use, but for seasoned men of understanding.

"Likewise must the deacons be grave, not doubletongued, not given to much wine, not greedy of filthy lucre; Holding the mystery of the faith in a pure conscience. And let these also first be proved; then let them use the office of a deacon, being found blameless. Even so must their wives be grave, not slanderers, sober, faithful in all things. Let the deacons be the husbands of one wife, ruling their children and their own houses well. For they that have used the office of a deacon well purchase to them-selves a good degree, and great boldness in the faith which is in Christ Jesus" (1Timothy 3:8–13).

The intention of these verses are clearly for that of a grown man with a wife and family, not that of an inexperienced little boy of age twelve. In the same token, an elder was not a young man of nineteen, but a mature, elderly person. Unlike our cul-ture where the aged are shut up in homes, the wise and the aged were highly valued leaders in the camp of the Lord. An elder was the source of wisdom and gray hair a crown of beauty to the aged. "The glory of young men is their strength: and the beauty of old men is the gray head" (Proverbs 20:29). Peter the apostle considered himself an elder: "The elders which are among you I exhort, who am also an elder, and a witness of the sufferings of Christ, and also a partaker of the glory that shall be revealed" (1 Peter 5:1).

Clearly, an elder is as the definition implies in the dictionary: an older person, an aged person, a forefather; ancestor; predecessor; an older person with some authority or dignity in a tribe or community.

# Chapter 12

## Articles of Faith Seven through Nine of the Church of Jesus Christ of Latter-day Saints

*Article 7. We believe in the gift of tongues, prophecy, revelation, visions, healing, interpretation of tongues, and so forth.*

*Article 8. We believe the Bible to be the word of God as far as it is translated correctly; we also believe the Book of Mormon to be the word of God.*

*Article 9. We believe all that God has revealed, all that He does now reveal, and we believe that He will yet reveal many great and important things pertaining to the Kingdom of God.*

## What Mormons Are Taught about the Gifts

Mormons are not much different than most churches on the topic of the gifts. However, Mormons in general only state this belief as it relates to Mormons who prophesy—those who have the gift of revelation, visions, and such. This is not to say that they accept any of these as valid outside of their priesthood authority, however (see the fifth Article of Faith).

The gift of tongues does not have universal agreement among Christian churches. Many views are held, some of which agree with the Mormon teaching on tongues. The Mormon viewpoint of tongues is that when someone speaks in their own native tongue, the Holy Spirit supernaturally interprets the words into the hearer's own native tongue or language.

This view, I feel, is part of a much deeper and powerful manifestation of the presence of the Holy Spirit in one's life. I will, however, leave this topic for others to define as it is beyond the scope of this book to defend or define this precious gift of God.

## What the Mormons are taught about prophecy and the scriptures

The gifts of prophecy, revelation, and visions among Mormons are taught to be of such high nature that a modern Mormon prophet's "revelation" supersedes the written word. The following is a quote from www.LDS.org on the subject:

This [Mormon] Church constantly needs the guidance of its head, the Lord and Savior, Jesus Christ. This was well taught by President George Q. Cannon, formerly a member of the First Presidency: "We have the Bible, the Book of Mormon and the Book of Doctrine and Covenants; but all these books, without the living oracles and a constant stream of revelation from the Lord, would not lead any people into the Celestial Kingdom of God. This may seem a strange declaration to make, but strange as it may sound, it is nevertheless true. "Of course, these records are all of infinite value. They cannot be too highly prized, nor can they be too closely studied. But in and of themselves, with all the light that they give, they are insufficient to guide the children of men and to lead them into the presence of God. To be thus led requires a living Priesthood and constant revelation from God to the people according to the circumstances in which they may be placed" (Gospel Truth: Discourses and Writings of President George Q. Cannon, 2 vols., sel. Jerreld L. Newquist, 1974, 1:323).

## Mormons are taught that the Bible is not translated correctly and therefore of lesser value than the Book of Mormon.

I find it of great interest that the Bible translation of Joseph Smith is not the official Bible used by the LDS church. Here again is some text taken from the site www.LDS.org.

"**The Joseph Smith Translation of the Bible:** With the restoration of divine priesthood authority and the reestablishment of the Church of Jesus Christ through the Prophet Joseph Smith, there came also the restoration of ancient scriptures. Not only were we to have a Bible, but also a Book of Mormon and other sacred records. The revelations received by the Prophet Joseph Smith made clear that the King James Version, great as it was, did not contain all that the ancient manuscripts had once contained. Many plain and precious things had been lost (see 1 Ne.13). It was not so much a matter of translation of languages, but also a faulty transmission of the text. The King James Version is thus a remarkable vestige of an even more remarkable record of the gospel that was preached anciently. With the Restoration, another revision of the English Bible was in order, not by a scholar but by a prophet. And it would come not from an ancient manuscript but from direct revelation of the same Lord from whom the Bible had originated. It was to be done at the Lord's commission rather than at the request of an earthly monarch or pope. This revision was to be an inspired version of the King James Bible, a divine restoration of ancient biblical knowledge. It is known today as the Inspired Version, or more properly, as the Joseph Smith Translation of the Bible. It should be seen in perspective as another step in the struggle to give mankind a Bible that not only can be read, but also can be understood. The Prophet Joseph Smith made his translation during the years 1830 to 1844."

## What does the Ninth Article of Faith mean?

When the church states that it believes "All that God has revealed, is revealing, and will reveal," it means Mormons believe all that God has (supposedly) revealed to the Mormon leadership, all that God is telling the Mormon leadership now, and all that God will give the Mormon leadership in the future. They also believe that these "new revelations" will become scripture, just as the apostles' words became scripture in the New Testament.

These new scriptures or revelations will then override anything that has been stated before the new revelation was received. Let's look closely at this statement from above: "But in and of themselves [the Bible and the Mormon scriptures], with all the light that they give, they are insufficient to guide the children of men and to lead them into the presence of God. To be thus led requires a living Priesthood and constant revelation from God to the people according to the circumstances in which they may be placed." Please consider what this means. In other words, it is not through the Word of God, it is not through faith in the Lord Jesus—it is only through the guidance of "modern day prophets" that a man can be exalted and be with God. While they may not make this direct claim, it is the essence or at least implication of what this statement really means if you follow the logic to its conclusion, based solely on their own words.

## We do not get to heaven but by one name—Jesus Christ.

Jesus said of Himself, "I am the way, the truth, and the life: no man cometh unto the Father, but by me" (John 14:6). When Jesus told the Jewish nation to search the scriptures, "for in them ye think ye have eternal life and they are they which testify of me" (John 5:39), He was only talking about the Torah, as the New Testament had not yet been written.

The written word of God was not, nor ever will be, subject to change by any "new revelation" of succeeding prophets. God's word is unchangeable. When God makes a decree of judgment, this decree can either be fulfilled or averted by repentance. On rare occasions in scripture, the prayer of intercession has touched God's heart and caused Him to postpone or even reverse a judgment. None of those things however, change the fact that His Word always stands. The Word of God has no "shadow of turning," and it is never subordinate to a successive new word. In fact, many of Christ's actions where done with these words on His lips: "That the scripture might be fulfilled."

If, then, Christ Himself would not, nor could, change the written Word, how can there be any credibility to the claim made by President George Q. Cannon that "without the living oracles and a constant stream of revelation from the Lord, would not lead any people into the Celestial Kingdom of God."?

If the written Word is not sufficient to save today, then it wasn't yesterday. Not even the New Testament changed a single thing other than to fulfill and to clarify what had already been written. In fact, not one word or punctuation mark was to be done away with, only fulfilled, according to Jesus.

## If God is unchanging, then why wouldn't He have prophets to whom He speaks now, just as in days of old? If He is unchanging, wouldn't that mean that new scriptures would need to be revealed till the end of time?

Please bear with me, friend, as this is a very detailed teaching. I have been asked this great question many times by members of the church, including my loving family. It is in reference to the ninth Article of Faith. The Mormon belief is that if God is the same "today, yesterday, and forever," then it must mean God will continue to reveal new truths. These new truths will then become the new scriptures for our day, just like in the days of the Bible. But in order to fully answer this question, we must first know why we are given scripture in the first place.

The problem arises with the premise of the question. If there is a flaw in the premise, there will always be a flaw in the conclusion. The fact that God is unchanging does not mean that things do not change. Lets look for example at Exodus 27:20–21:

"And thou shalt command the children of Israel, that they bring thee pure olive oil beaten for the light, to cause the lamp to burn always. In the tabernacle of the congregation without the veil, which is before the testimony, Aaron and his sons shall order it from evening to morning before the LORD: it shall be a statute for ever unto their generations on the behalf of the children of Israel."

This is just one of many examples I could mention that would illustrate my point that, while God is unchangeable, His words do have a purpose. The purpose of the spoken Word, once achieved, brings fulfillment to His word. If this were not so, we would still be burning incense in the temple night and day and bringing burnt offerings.

Mormons quote a passage from the Book of Mormon that tells them that God will always bring new scripture to light. The verse reads, "a Bible, a Bible. We have a Bible, and there can be no more Bible." They say this because we in the Christian faith hold to the Bible as the completed Word of God.

## Why we don't need new scriptures.

The Word of God is not some random set of events recorded by man, but are a guide to eternal life. It starts out with the origin of the earth and life upon it. It shows the fall of mankind and gives the promise of a Savior. It sets forth the ways of eternal life. The law of God is the guide that shows mankind his need for salvation through atonement in order to be reconciled with God. The law came in to show us just how great our need was, and how impossible to achieve our goal by our own efforts to become holy.

**Romans 5:20:** Moreover the law entered, that the offence might abound. But where sin abounded, grace did much more abound.

**Romans 7:12–13:** Wherefore the law is holy, and the commandment holy, and just, and good. Was then that which is good made death unto me? God forbid. But sin, that it might appear sin, working death in me by that which is good; that sin by the commandment might become exceeding sinful.

The law of God stands forever unchangeable. The law was not done away with new revelation but fulfilled with the higher law of the Spirit.

Whereas the law was written on stone and dealt with the outward ordinances of the flesh, the new covenant law was written on the heart. It fulfilled this first law and raised it to a higher plane—that of the spirit man. Just as the heavens are higher than the earth and God's thoughts higher than our thoughts, the law of grace is higher than that of the law of the commandments.

We, therefore, no longer need new revelation on how to properly sacrifice a bull, a goat, or a lamb, because that portion was completed in full when a higher sacrifice was offered that was so complete, no further or higher sacrifice could be offered. It was a sacrifice so sufficient that it completed the very purpose of all sacrifices, which was to cover sin in order to gain access to God.

Nothing sinful can be in His presence; therefore anything unclean would be destroyed if brought before Him. Yet, this sacrifice had the power to make complete access to God forever possible, even for us whose righteousness is "as filthy rags" (Isaiah 64:6).

The Law was given to show mankind how to be clean in order to return to God's presence, as in the garden. It pointed out the fact that we could not make it on our own; it showed us just how sinful we had become. The blood of the sacrifice of the old covenant covered our sin in order to regain access to the presence of God, but it was not sufficient, first because of our continued sin, and second because of the insufficiency of the blood of sinless animals to cover our sin. Therefore, that old covenant we call the "Old Testament" was completed when a higher, more complete sacrifice came because everything that was needed to point to the true atonement—to make us at one with God—was set forth.

When the Lamb of God came in the flesh, He died, He rose on the third day, and then He was set on high. The apostles were then given the assignment to be the special witnesses of all that they had both seen and heard the Lord do and of His resurrection from the dead.

**Acts 1:22:** Beginning from the baptism of John, unto that same day that he was taken up from us, must one be ordained to be a witness with us of his resurrection.

**Luke 24:46–49:** And said unto them, Thus it is written, and thus it behooved Christ to suffer, and to rise from the dead the third day: And that repentance and remission of sins should be preached in his name among all nations, beginning at Jerusalem. And ye are witnesses of these things. And, behold, I send the promise of my Father upon you: but tarry ye in the city of Jerusalem, until ye be endued with power from on high.

These special witnesses were given the same Word of God voice as were the prophets of old, because the gospel was to be taught in all the world and the same grace was to be given to the Gentiles as was to the Jews.

This order of things had to be in place because Jesus's mission was to the lost sheep of Israel. The message had to be first offered to the children of Israel: "These twelve Jesus sent forth, and commanded them, saying, Go not into the way of the Gentiles, and into any city of the Samaritans enter ye not: but go rather to the lost sheep of the house of Israel" (Matthew 10:5–6). After Jesus's resurrection, with this commandment having been fulfilled, He sent them into all the world: "Go ye therefore, and teach all nations, baptizing them in the name of the Father, and of the Son, and of the Holy Ghost" (Matthew 28:19).

The Lord upon His ascension promised that the Comforter would come. Later, the further revelation of the grace that was to be given to the Gentiles would come. Each of these actions were to be recorded as scripture because they brought us closer and closer to full communion with God.

In the same way that the Old Covenant had its fulfillment in Christ, the New Covenant (the New Testament) had its fulfillment—or rather became "finished"—in the fullness of the revelation to the Gentiles and the Revelation of Jesus Christ, where His full eventual triumph was shown in "dark speeches" (King James language for "in a mystery"). The purpose of the Bible and specifically the New Testament was to show how Jesus had fulfilled the Law. It is the gospel, the good news, and it is finished because God has given the full revelation of His Son and the Son's bride, the true church of God. This bride or church would not be comprised of the Israel of the flesh, but the Israel of the Spirit through the choice of God.

In Christ, we were given the full revelation on how to be reconciled to God, and even further the whole of creation would also be reconciled and brought back to the perfect state it once enjoyed. This time however, it would be on a higher, heavenly existence.

This is why we no longer need any new revelation to reconcile us. This is why the Bible is more than sufficient to save us. This is why through the power of God this salvation is so simple and complete that we don't even need a perfect translation. However you say this: "Jesus Christ and Him crucified," you are telling the good news. Jesus took upon Him our sins, He is risen by the power of the Most High God. If this meaning shines through, no matter how it is translated, you have the fullness of the revelation.

## All these things have an end.

The Mormons claim that there will always be new scripture, but the Word of God plainly states that all prophecy, gifts, and the like are only for a season. When Christ returns, we will not need new scripture to tell us the Word of God, as we will be with the Word of God. Not only will we be with Him, but we shall know all things. All things that the Father has given to the Son will be ours. Praise the Lord!

"For we know in part, and we prophesy in part. But when that which is perfect is come, then that which is in part shall be done away. When I was a child, I spake as a child, I understood as a child, I thought as a child: but when I became a man, I put away childish things. For now we see through a glass, darkly; but then face to face: now I know in part; but then shall I know even as also I am known" (1 Corinthians 13:9–12).

When we are looking face to face with the Lamb of God, we will not need to ask "What saith the Father," because we will have been given all that the Father has.

Oh my dear Mormon friends, please understand that the gifts of God are so much more than you have been told. The depth of salvation is so much more complete than we can imagine. The realms of Heaven will be such a wonder, that to gaze at the Lord night and day will not be boring or a trite experience that could become dull or fail to bring eternal joy. There are beasts that surround the throne of God every minute of every day, saying "Holy, holy, holy, LORD God Almighty, which was, and is, and is to come" (Revelation 4:8).

In my weakness, I have praised the Lord for a whole night, but then I'm ready to do something else. I believe these "beasts" around the throne are saying "Holy, holy, holy" night and day because the wonder of God is fresh and new each time; each word spoken is a result of a new aspect of God that was before unseen. Each expression is, not a mere multiplying of words, but a fresh utterance of wonder only realized new that second.

Oh Lord, how holy is Your name, how awesome Your salvation, how complete, how perfect your Word!

Without hesitation or shame, yes, my dear Mormon friend, we do say we have a Bible, and it is complete. Next, we shall see the Son of Man coming in the clouds with great glory. Soon we shall understand and know for ourselves the mysteries of God. The gospel is complete, the covenant between God and man is clearly laid out before the eyes of all men by the Holy Spirit.

**You don't need any man to stand between you and God; you don't need a new Moses or any new scripture when you have Jesus.**

# Chapter 13

## Articles Ten through thirteen of the Church of Jesus Christ of Latter-day Saints.

*Article 10. We believe in the literal gathering of Israel and in the restoration of the Ten Tribes; that Zion (the New Jerusalem) will be built upon the American continent; that Christ will reign personally upon the earth; and that the earth will be renewed and receive its paradisiacal glory.*

*Article 11. We claim the privilege of worshiping Almighty God according to the dictates of our own conscience, and allow all men the same privilege, let them worship how, where, or what they may.*

*Article 12. We believe in being subject to kings, presidents, rulers, and magistrates, in obeying, honoring, and sustaining the law.*

*Article 13. We believe in being honest, true, chaste, benevolent, virtuous, and in doing good to all men; indeed, we may say that we follow the admonition of Paul—*

*We believe all things, we hope all things, we have endured many things, and hope to be able to endure all things. If there is anything virtuous, lovely, or of good report or praiseworthy, we seek after these things.*

THIS CHAPTER WILL conclude our examination of the Mormon Articles of Faith. We will begin with the text of Article 10, which needs little clarification as it clearly states what Mormons believe. Let's go straight to what the Bible teaches about the gathering of the lost tribes of Israel and the coming of the New Jerusalem.

## The gathering of Israel

The Bible states that to be of Israel is not based on the actual family tree that is now dispersed throughout the entire world through mixed or interracial marriages.

While not an official teaching of the Mormon church, it is widely speculated among the members that the "lost tribes" are living underground in the center of the earth. Or that they are hiding out in some remote part of the world. It is not surprising that they would think this, as it is the only way a lost tribe could exist without being infiltrated by outside blood or remain hidden in this modern age of satellites and technology.

Unsubstantiated thinking like this is the backbone of the church's stronghold on the minds of its people. The leaders make a statement, then the church is charged with the duty to accept it.

## Where are the lost tribes then?

God has dispersed the tribes throughout the bloodline of humanity. To be in one of the tribes of Israel is not merely to be born into that bloodline. It is only for those whose faith was of that of Abraham. Consider the words of Romans 9:6–8:

"Not as though the word of God hath taken none effect. For they are not all Israel, which are of Israel: Neither, because they are the seed of Abraham, are they all children: but in Isaac shall thy seed be called. That is, they which are the children of the flesh, these are not the children of God: but the children of the promise are counted for the seed."

Because of these verses, we can see that the "lost tribes" are not the Israel that the Bible refers to. This is not to say there are not people who may have a more pure bloodline, or perhaps even a microscopic chance that direct, pure-blooded descendants may exist. While I do believe that God honors the bloodline of Israel when they turn to Him, this possibility is not really the question, as we learned in Romans 9: 6. They are not all Israel because of genealogies—the true "tribes of Israel" are those that are Israel inwardly by promise and not by bloodline.

The lost tribes, therefore, are not lost whatsoever. They are just as Jesus said of the kingdom of God: "And when he was demanded of the Pharisees, when the kingdom of God should come, he answered them and said, The kingdom of God cometh not with observation: Neither shall they say, Lo here! or, lo there! for, behold, the kingdom of God is within you" (Luke 17:20–21).

The ten tribes are not going to come marching over the hill (or out of it). Theories abound of how the Israelites are actually those of African heritage, the Japanese, and others. Truthfully, I don't know, But I contest that it does not matter. The promise is to the seed of Abraham. The true seed of Abraham are those who carry the faith of Abraham: "And if ye be Christ's, then are ye Abraham's seed, and heirs according to the promise (Galatians 3:29).

We know that the promise of the return of the ten tribes is not literal, because Israel is of Abraham's seed and the seed of Abraham is not accounted, according to the Bible, by the flesh but by faith in the true Jesus Christ of the Bible.

## The "New Jerusalem"

"Now therefore in the sight of all Israel the congregation of the LORD, and in the audience of our God, keep and seek for all the commandments of the LORD your God: that ye may possess this good land, and leave it for an inheritance for your children after you for ever" (1 Chronicles 28:8).

The whole of the covenant that God made with Abraham began with the promise of the specific land of Canaan, recorded in Genesis 17:7–9.

"And I will establish my covenant between me and thee and thy seed after thee in their generations for an everlasting covenant, to be a God unto thee, and to thy seed after thee. And I will give unto thee, and to thy seed after thee, the land wherein thou art a stranger, all the land of Canaan, for an everlasting possession; and I will be their God. And God said unto Abraham, Thou shalt keep my covenant therefore, thou, and thy seed after thee in their generations."

When the people of God were commanded to pray, it was toward this specific piece of land. Yet, and even more importantly, the Bible states that the "New Jerusalem" comes down from heaven. While this fact is not denied by Mormon theology, the biblical truth is that according to the promise of God to Abraham, it must reside in the land of Canaan.

The Bible is in agreement that the Earth will be renewed, as the Mormons also teach, and that the new city of God will be a wonder beyond comprehension of our earthly minds.

## Articles 11 and 12.

Let's review the text of these Articles of Faith.

**Article 11.** We claim the privilege of worshiping Almighty God according to the dictates of our own conscience and allow all men the same privilege; let them worship how, where, or what they may.

**Article 12.** We believe in being subject to kings, presidents, rulers, and magistrates, in obeying, honoring, and sustaining the law.

These are two wonderful statements that all people of all races, religions, and creeds should follow. They are also one of many reasons that the people of the Mormon faith are some of the most productive, honorable people around.

I attest that the people of the Mormon faith, as a whole, live by these fine principles. These are not mere empty words. These statements are not original to the Mormons, however. The Word of God says the same. As stated in the beginning of this book, "all truth is true, no matter where you find it." The Bible, therefore, does not agree with this teaching. This teaching agrees with the Bible. Romans 13:1–5 teaches us to

"Let every soul be subject unto the higher powers. For there is no power but of God: the powers that be are ordained of God. Whosoever therefore resisteth the power, resisteth the ordinance of God: and they that resist shall receive to themselves damnation. For rulers are not a terror to good works, but to the evil. Wilt thou then not be afraid of the power? do that which is good, and thou shalt have praise of the same: For he is the minister of God to thee for good. But if thou do that which is evil, be afraid; for he beareth not the sword in vain: for he is the minister of God, a revenger to execute wrath upon him that doeth evil. Wherefore ye must needs be subject, not only for wrath, but also for conscience sake."

## Article 13.

**Article 13.** *We believe in being honest, true, chaste, benevolent, virtuous, and in doing good to all men; indeed, we may say that we follow the admonition of Paul—We believe all things, we hope all things, we have endured many things, and hope to be able to endure all things. If there is anything virtuous, lovely, or of good report or praiseworthy, we seek after these things.*

Again, this statement agrees with the Bible. The only issue I have with it is that, according to Mormon teaching, these beautiful things that help keep a Christian's walk pure and effective are also necessary for salvation and part of the works they feel must be performed in order to earn salvation or to be found "worthy." Romans 10:3 calls this "establishing their own righteousness." Consider the words of Romans 10:2–4:

For I bear them record that they have a zeal of God, but not according to knowledge. For they being ignorant of God's righteousness, and going about to establish their own righteousness, have not submitted themselves unto the righteousness of God. For Christ is the end of the law for righteousness to everyone that believeth.

The wonderful people of the Mormon faith should be honored, loved, and their rights respected. They have every right to worship according to what they perceive as truth. Being raised with them, however, I testify and agree with the record found in Romans that they, like the Jews of old, "have a zeal for God, but not according to knowledge." While their righteousness is a wonderful thing in this dark, ugly world, it cannot, alone, save them.

# Chapter 14

## A Typical Christian Statement of Faith

*For I determined not to know any thing among you,*
*save Jesus Christ, and him crucified.*

*1 CORINTHIANS 2:2*

*I*N THIS CHAPTER I will attempt to give an overview of what some Christian churches agree upon as the key elements of the faith. This, of course, is not all-inclusive, nor do I feel it must be. The following is a typical statement of faith from a Bible-believing, doctrinally sound church. I do not endorse any one denomination other than Christianity itself, that holds to at least these basic principles. Please note that these are not my words but rather an anonymously given statement of faith by a large Christian Church, and only given as an example.

1. **The Doctrine of the Scriptures**
   A. We believe the holy scriptures of the Old and New Testaments to be inerrant as originally written and God-breathed to Spirit-controlled men. (2 Timothy 3:16–17; 2 Peter 1:19–21)
   B. We believe that the scriptures (the Old and New Testaments) are absolutely the only authority for the Christian in matters of faith and practice. (Colossians

1:10; Matthew 4:4, 7, 10; 2 Peter 3:18; 1 Peter 2:2; Romans 1:16–17)

## 2. The Doctrine of God
### A. Essential Being of God
1. God is spirit. (John 4:24; 2 Corinthians 3:17)
2. God is invisible to man. (Exodus 33:20; John 1:18; 1 John 4:12)
3. God is living God. (Jeremiah 10:10; 1 Thessalonians 1:19

### B. Attributes of God
1) Self-existent. The existence of God is in Himself (Exodus 3:14, 6:3, 1 Timothy 1:17; John 5:26)
2) Infinite. God has no limits or bounds. (Job 11:7–9; Romans 11:33)
3) Omnipresent. God is everywhere; He fills the universe (Psalm 139:7–10; Acts 17:27)
4) Omniscient. God knows everything. (Psalm 147:5; Hebrews 4:13)
5) Omnipotent. God is able to do whatever He wills. (Matthew 19:26; Daniel 4:35)
6) Immutable. God is unchangeable. (Psalm 102:27; James 1:17)

### C. Trinity of God
1) We believe in one God, eternally existing in three Persons; God the Father, God the Son, God the Holy Spirit. (Father: John 6:27) (Son: John 1:1, 18; Titus 2:12–13) (Holy Spirit: Acts 5:3–4)
2) We believe in the unity of the Trinity. (Deut. 6:4; Isa. 48:16; Matt. 28:19; I Tim.2:5)

### D. The Person of Jesus Christ
1) We believe in the preexistence of Jesus Christ. Christ is without beginning and end. (Micah 5:2; John 1:1, 14; 17:5; Revelation 1:8)
2) We believe that Christ is deity and that He never ceased to be God for one instant; Christ in the human

realm did not lay aside His deity. (John 1:18; Titus 2:13; Heb. 13: 6; I Tim. 2:5)

3. **The Humanity of Christ**
   A. **He Was Truly Man as if He Had Never Been God**
      1) He was born of a virgin. (Matthew 1:25; Luke 1:26–38)
      2) He had human weakness. (John 4:6; 19:28)
      3) He had human development. (Luke 2: 52)
   B. **The Work of Christ**
      1) We believe that the Lord Jesus Christ accomplished our redemption through His death on the cross as a representative for us, He was a vicarious, substitutionary sacrifice; and all who believe in Him are justified solely on the basis of His shed blood. (Romans 3:21–25; 1 John 2:1–2; 1 Timothy 2:5–6)
      2) We believe that the purpose of the atoning death of Jesus Christ was to satisfy the justice of God (Romans 3:26; Isaiah 53:10), and to give us forgiveness of sins and new life. (Ephesians 1:7; 1 John 2:1–2)
      3) We believe that the object of His atoning death was for:
         a) The whole world (John 3:16, Colossians 1:20; 1 John 2:1–2; 1 Timothy 2:4–6; 2 Peter 3:9)
         b) The church (Ephesians 5:25)
         c) The individual (Galatians 2:20)
   C. **The Resurrection of Christ**
      1) We believe that Christ was raised bodily from the grave on the third day (1 Corinthians 15:4; Ephesians 1:20) and it was God who raised Him. (Acts 2:24)
      2) We believe that it was the same body in a glorified state. (Luke 24:13–25; John 20:26–29)
   D. **The Present Ministries of Christ**
      1) We believe that the Lord Jesus Christ ascended into heaven and is now exalted at the right hand of God, where, as our High Priest, He fulfills the ministries of Representative, Intercessor and Advocate. (Acts

1:9–10; Hebrews 7:25; 9:24; Romans 8:34; 1 John 2:1–2; 1 Timothy 2:5)

   2) We believe that the Lord Jesus Christ is the head of the church. (Ephesians 1:20–23)

   3) We believe that the Lord Jesus Christ is the Shepherd and Bishop of our souls. (1 Peter 2:25)

   4) The Doctrine of the Holy Spirit

## 4. The Person of the Holy Spirit

  A. We believe in the deity and personality of the Holy Spirit (Ephesians 4:30; 1 Thessalonians 5:19; Acts 5:3–4, 9; John 15:26)

    1) The work of the Holy Spirit

    2) We believe that the Holy Spirit convicts the whole world of sin, righteousness, and judgment. (John 16:8–11)

    3) We believe that He is the supernatural agent in regeneration. (2 Thessalonians 2:13; 1 Peter 1:2)

    4) We believe He baptizes all believers into the body of Christ. (1 Corinthians 12:12–14; 6:19)

    5) We believe He indwells and seals believers unto the day of redemption. (1 Corinthians 6:19; Romans 8:16; Ephesians1:13–14; 4:30)

## 5. The Doctrine of Man

  A. The origin

    1) We believe that man, in the person of the first Adam, was created innocent but voluntarily sinned. (Genesis 3)

    2) We believe that this transgression plunged the race into condemnation and death resulting in man's being shaped in iniquity and born in sin and becoming a practical sinner with the first expression of personal choice, not by constraint but by choice, and

so is without excuse before God. (Romans 5:10–19; Ephesians 2:1–2; Genesis 3; Romans 1:18–32)

3) We believe that no person can be saved apart from hearing the message of salvation and believing in Christ. (Romans 1:20; Acts 4:12)

## 6. The Doctrine of Sin

A. We believe that sin entered the human race by Adam's voluntary sin, placing all the human race in sin at our physical birth. (Genesis 3:6–13; Romans 3:9–10, 23; 5:12; Ephesians 2:3)

B. We believe that sin entered the angelic world first when Lucifer fell. (Isaiah 14:12–17; Genesis 3:1–6; Ezekiel 28:11–15; 2 Corinthians 11:14; Revelation 12:9, 14–15; John 8:44)

## 7. The Doctrine of Salvation

A. We believe that God sovereignly selected out the plan and the person according to His grace and mercy but did not violate man's responsibility. (Acts 2:23; Romans 10:9–10; John 6:27; Ephesians 1:4; 2 Thessalonians 2:13; 1 Peter 2:2–2)

B. We believe that faith in the finished work of the Lord Jesus Christ is the only condition of salvation from sin and the salvation is wholly secure. (Acts 16:31; Ephesians 2:8–9; Titus 3: 5–7; John 3:16)

C. We believe that all who take Christ as their Savior are born from above and are kept by God's power and are eternally secure in Christ. (John 10:28–29; Romans 8:35–39; Ephesians 1:13–14; 1 John 5:11–13)

## 8. The Believer's Walk or Daily Conduct in the World

A. We believe that the Bible alone provides the guiding principles for faith and practice. (Romans 10:17; 1 John 2:6; 2 Timothy 2:15; 3:16–17; 1 Peter 2:2; Colossians 4:6)

B. We believe that the believer should seek to read and fulfill the church covenant as stated. (Colossians 4:6; 2 Timothy 2:15; 1 Peter 3:15)

C. We believe that whatsoever you do, do it heartily as unto the Lord as we share and show our faith both verbally and outwardly. (Ephesians 5:16–17; Colossians 3:17, 23; Philippians 2:15–16; James 1:22; 2:17, 20, 26)

9. **The Doctrine of the Church**

A. We believe that the church universal is a New Testament institution, established by Jesus Christ, who is the sole Head, and will be consummated at the second coming of Christ when we will all come to the unity of the faith. (Matthew 16:18; Ephesians 1:22; 5:23–33; 1 Thessalonians 4:13–18)

B. We believe that the church universal is manifested through the life of the true believer and is not merely a local church, which is a congregation of believers. (Matthew 8:15–17; 1 Corinthians 1:2; 6:4–5; 7:17; 11:16; 1 Timothy 3:1–15: Romans 12:5; Ephesians 2:19–22)

C. Our position as a local body. We believe in fellowship with other Bible-believing churches holding forth historic, strictly Bible-based Christianity. We believe in separation from apostasy. We believe the scriptures admonish us not to participate with other churches in services, associates, and campaigns that are not Bible-believing. (2 Corinthians 6:11–7:1; Ephesians 5:7; 2 Thessalonians 3:1–6, 14)

# Beliefs of a biblically sound Christian church.

1. Jesus was born of a virgin.
2. Jesus is Immanuel, God with us.
3. Salvation is apart from works and is only achieved by a true statement of faith and belief in the heart resulting in right living. Because indeed, faith without works is dead.

4. God is Elohim, meaning that He has eternally existed as "the Gods" Typically know as the Trinity; Father, Son and Holy Ghost, three in one.

5. Jesus was both fully God, and fully man and in Him is the fullness of God. We, therefore, worship God through Jesus as the incarnation of the Father, Son and Holy Ghost.

6. All true believers that call on the name of God will seek to obey Him in all things.

7. Jesus Christ is the End of the Law to all who believe and are called according to His purposes.

8. Many churches also believe, as do I, that believers will be filled with the Holy Ghost and will speak with other tongues as the Spirit gives them utterance. I am also in agreement with the many that hold that this is also only a matter of sanctification and not salvation.

I do not consider those who believe that speaking in tongues is a prerequisite of salvation are unsaved, even if they incorrectly hold this belief in regard to others, including me. Here is another statement of faith from a typical Pentecostal church.

1. We believe the Bible is the inspired and only infallible and authoritative written Word of God.

2. We believe there is one God, eternally existent in three persons: God the Father, God the Son and God the Holy Spirit.

3. We believe in the deity of our Lord Jesus Christ, in His virgin birth, in His sinless life, in His miracles, in His vicarious and atoning death, in His bodily resurrection, in His ascension to the right hand of the Father, in His personal future return to this earth in power and glory to rule a thousand years.

4. We believe in the Blessed Hope—the rapture of the church at Christ's coming.

5. We believe that the only means of being cleansed from sin is through repentance and faith in the precious blood of Christ.

6. We believe the regeneration by the Holy Spirit is absolutely essential for personal salvation.

7. We believe that the redemptive work of Christ on the cross provides healing of the human body in answer to prayer.

8. We believe that the baptism in the Holy Spirit, according to Acts 2:4, is given to believers who ask for it.

9. We believe in the sanctifying power of the Holy Spirit by whose indwelling the Christian is enabled to live a holy life.

10. We believe in the resurrection of both the saved and the lost, the one to everlasting life and the other to everlasting damnation.

By now it should be evident that many biblically valid churches hold many basic principle in common.

# Chapter 15

## Witnessing to a Mormon

### What not to do

While I am hopeful this first section does not come across too harshly, I feel very strongly about this and hope that it will be received in the spirit of love that it is meant.

I want to talk to all my Christian brothers and sisters out there who have a heart to help. Please know that standing at the temple grounds yelling at people, as I have seen some do, is playing right into the hands of the enemy. I say this because such actions are the very things that feed the persecution complex many Mormons experience.

If you love them so much that you want to share the truth with them, then be a real friend. Don't dishonor the name of the Lord with bitter words; don't dishonor the faith by denying a fellow citizen of this great nation the right to worship in peace. Do things the way Christ did—with love, compassion, healing, and teaching. These are the things that set the tone for truth to be received. Ultimately it is the work of the Spirit, not men that converts a heart.

Every decent person knows you can say all the right things in the wrong way and be less than effective. You may walk away feeling like you did your "Christian duty," but most likely you just pushed someone farther from reach. A person who does this must not understand the false sense of security "knowing" you are in "the only true church on earth" can give a Mormon. They aren't going to give up this assurance because you yelled at them. The Word of God, in John 8:32, says: "ye shall know the truth and the truth shall set you free."

It is the truth of God's Word witnessed to us by the Holy Spirit that sets us free, not angry words thrown at people. Too often, you look like an enemy. You come with the guns of hostility, not with the bread of life and peace as a concerned friend.

I wonder why these well-meaning folk don't first stop in Palestine and go to a Muslim holy site? Why don't they yell the truth of God's Word at them, with all their courage? How long would you last? No one does this there, because they would be stoned or beheaded. If we don't do that, then why do we treat our own fellow citizens with less respect? Is it only because they are a meek people? It is my hope that such a one would stay home and learn some compassion, love, meekness, and tenderness before you start your quest.

## What about the inconsistencies in teaching between different churches?

Joseph Smith taught in his first vision that God was unhappy with all the churches on the earth because they don't all agree. In the things of God, we are like very young children trying to understand the deeper meaning of quantum physics. When this life is over, we will find that in our wisest, most insightful scholarship, we only saw darkly as through an imperfect glass while here on earth (1 Corinthians 13:12).

With the differences of opinion by which many would separate themselves from one another and cry "heresy," I find no biblical evidence or justification for true Christians to question each other's biblically based salvation based solely on non-atoning points of doctrine.

**While we love to be around people that are like-minded, there is only one true church on the earth.**

The Bible makes it clear that there is only one true church—the Bride of Christ—on the earth. Ephesians 4:1–7 says:

I therefore, the prisoner of the Lord, beseech you that ye walk worthy of the vocation wherewith ye are called, with all lowliness and meekness, with longsuffering, forbearing one another in love; endeavouring to keep the unity of the Spirit in the bond of peace. There is one body, and one Spirit, even as ye are called in one hope of your calling; One Lord, one faith, one baptism, one God and Father of all, who is above all, and through all, and in you all. But unto every one of us is given grace according to the measure of the gift of Christ.

Let's look closely at verse 7. Each one of us is given the measure of faith. However, not everyone has the same willingness to walk in measures beyond what faith they can understand. There are those who can receive the idea of salvation in truth, but have a hard time believing—for instance, that God really hears and answers prays for healing.

This does not make them any less Christian, but it may limit their experience of the richness and power of God. It may lead them to fellowship with others who feel this same way. All Christian faiths that believe in the biblical Jesus and call on His name for salvation are saved according to the Bible. Even if we feel that we alone are correct, it does not change the truth that salvation comes from faith in Jesus alone.

In addition, the church is not a place with seats and a pulpit. The Church is the people of God. God's people are scattered as the lost tribes throughout all Christian denominations. The people of God are His true believers. Many will say the right prayer, will even believe the right stuff, but never truly convert to the Lord. Some never really "believe in their hearts" that God raised Jesus from the dead; at least not the real Jesus.

There is no denomination that can lay claim to all of God's truth. This is because, no matter how true our beliefs may be, we are not true. We, the true church of God, are sinners striving for perfection. We do this, not merely to apprehend that by which we were apprehended, but because any true believer is going to live a holy lifestyle out of love for the Lord. If one does not follow after right living, they may not be Christians and should follow the admonition of Paul in 2 Corinthians 13:5–6: "Examine yourselves, whether ye be in the faith; prove your own selves. Know ye not your own selves, how that Jesus Christ is in you, except ye be reprobates? But I trust that ye shall know that we are not reprobates." (Reprobates are those that have been rejected due to unbelief.)

We are wholly unfit to judge the heart of mankind. We don't know what is behind the actions of a person, nor the level of faith they walk in. Christian churches make mistakes—they are wrong about some things, but they each teach a level of faith that is more or less in harmony with the Word of God. This is why we cannot rely on the teachers of man for our salvation. May our goal be that of 1 Corinthians 2:4–5: "My speech and my preaching was not with enticing words of man's wisdom, but in demonstration of the Spirit and of power: That your faith should not stand in the wisdom of men, but in the power of God."

## Do not forsake the assembling together.

We need to find like-minded believers to be in fellowship with, but this does not mean that we are looking to these men and woman to tell us what everything means. Instead, we should be pointing each other to the Word of God. It is the duty of every "overseer" to be merely a servant and a road sign, pointing all toward the Lord Jesus and His word, not just their own prophecies and teachings.

## Then how does one come to the Lord?

I'm so glad you asked. Witnessing to a Mormon is the same as witnessing to anyone. Regardless of the fact that a Mormon has been groomed to refute the truth, it is the truth that sets us free. I have found that even though a Mormon will recite to you all the verses they have been taught to disprove your proof, if they are true seekers, they will hear the truth.

The Word of God always accomplishes the thing it was sent to do. Just speak the truth and let God do the converting. Many times I have talked to people who deny everything I say. Then, God Himself in His own time witnesses to them the truth of His Word, apart from my "wise" counsel.

## Here are some key scriptures to lead one to salvation

**Romans 3:23**—Everyone sins.

**Romans 3:10**—No one is "good."

**Romans 6:23**—We earned the death sentence.

**John 3:3**—You must be "born again."

**John 1:12**—Those who receive Him are given the power to become "sons of God."

**Romans 10:9–11**—We receive Him by a confession of faith and true belief in the heart that leads unto right living.

**2 Corinthians 5:15**—After we receive Him, our life is no longer our own. We do not have the right to live life for our own pleasure, but we live for the pleasure of God.

**Revelation 3:20**—God wants a personal, sit-down-to-a-meal-together relationship with each of us. He will not barge into our lives, however. He "stands at the door" of our hearts, knocking; we must invite Him in.

## Confession of faith:

If you have been touched by the words of this book and want to begin a new relationship with God, to have all your sins forgiven, and to be free for all time, it starts with a confession of faith. Pray words like these below from your heart, and God will hear you, and you will be born again from on high.

Lord Jesus, I realize that I am a sinner, and apart from You, I have no hope of salvation. I believe that You, Jesus, are the Son of God, and that God raised You from the dead. I believe that I can only be saved by faith in the finished work of Christ on the cross and not by my own acts of righteousness. I ask You, Lord Jesus, to come into my life and save me from my sin. I surrender my whole life to You and commit to live a holy life for Your glory. I believe I can only achieve this by your grace. Thank you, God, for saving me. In the name of Jesus Christ I pray. Amen (so be it).

If you believed in your heart these words you just prayed, you are saved! You will now begin a lifelong journey toward "sanctification" in which your life is set aside for holy use.

The more you submit to this process through diligent scripture study, prayer, and faithful living according to the commandments of God, the more your life will line up with the will of God. The more your life lines up with the will of God, the more you will be used for His glory and the more peace you will feel.

If you resist the sanctification process, you will be unhappy and be walking away from the blessings of the Lord. While God will never leave you, while you can never lose this free gift of salvation, you most assuredly can lose your peace and your reward.

The wages of sin are always death. If you continue to sin willfully, you will be sowing the seeds of death in your life and call into question your true belief in Christ. Everyone who truly believes turns away from sin.

You will make mistakes; you will falter—but God is just and holy to forgive and to cleanse us from all unrighteousness. If you make unwise choices with your health, for instance, salvation will not make you skinny, healthy, and wise. It will give you the ability however, to submit to the process that you were once unable to achieve by your own acts of righteousness.

Find a Bible-believing church to attend where you can serve and give. Remember the Word of God says "iron sharpens iron" (Proverbs 27:17). The sharpening process is based on friction. We are going to rub each other wrong. Meeting with the church is a way to be refined as we bear with each other's burdens and faults. Do not shun this process as, within this friction, you will become a more useful tool in the hands of God.

Always remember as you seek for a church to fellowship with, all cults have a few things in common:

1. They will always question the deity of Christ.

2. They will always question the finality of God's Word, the Bible.

3. They will try to usurp the power of Christ and rule and Lord over you with their doctrine.

A true man of God talks more about the power and authority of the Lord than his or her own authority to act in His name. Trust in the Lord, and He will guide you and order your every step. Remember the words of Psalm 37:23—'The steps of a good man are ordered by the Lord: and he delighteth in his way."

# $\mathcal{A}$PPENDIX

As a note to my Mormon friends I hope you will consider that while it is common practice to disregard the "non-official teachings" from the book *Mormon Doctrine*, by McConkie, any long-term member knows that this book, or at least the teaching it contains, was, and is, quoted heavily to this day in LDS church meetings across the globe.

McConkie did not make up the statements contained in the book. He quoted recognized doctrinal church authorities including, Joseph Smith, Brigham Young, Orson Pratt, John Taylor, and even his contemporary prophet and leader, Joseph Fielding Smith.

It has been the long-term tendency of the church to choose which teachings of their beloved leaders are inspired and which are not. Those that cause controversy are deemed unofficial. This includes teaching from Joseph Smith himself. It has been my observation, however, that these teachings are highly regarded among the leaders and teachers of the church. I personally heard these statements throughout my life as a Mormon for the first thirty-three years of my life.

# *B* I B L I O G R A P H Y :

ALL BIBLE QUOTES and paraphrases from the KJV of the Bible
All other sources are stated here and within the text and from my own eye witness accounts in LDS churches I've attended in many places all over the US and Europe.

Chapter one:

God preserves a remnant and His word: Consider the great prophet Elijah, who felt that he was the only true believer left on earth. However, God had reserved unto Himself, seven thousand men that had not bowed to Baal (1 Kings 19:18).

Consider the words of Isaiah 40:22. "It is he that sitteth upon the circle of the earth, and the inhabitants thereof are as grasshoppers; that stretcheth out the heavens as a curtain, and spreadeth them out as a tent to dwell in."

Due to unbelief God degreed: "And he said go, and tell this people, hear ye indeed, but understand not, and see ye indeed, but perceive not" (Isaiah 6:9).

Chapter two:

"whatsoever a man soweth, that shall he also reap" (Galatians 6:7)

"If you do good, you do good for yourselves; and if you do evil, [you do it] to yourselves" (Qur'an 17:7).

John Taylor, an early church leader stated: "Joseph Smith, the Prophet and Seer of the Lord, has done more, save Jesus only, for the salvation of men in this world, than any other man that ever lived in it. In the short space of twenty years, he has brought forth the Book of Mormon, which he translated by the gift and power of God, and has been the means of publishing it on two continents; has sent the fullness of the everlasting gospel, which it contained, to the four quarters of the earth; has brought forth the revelations and commandments which compose this book of Doctrine and Covenants, and many other wise documents and instructions for the benefit of the children of men; gathered many thousands of the Latter-day Saints, founded a great city, and left a fame and name that cannot be slain. He lived great, and he died great in the eyes of God and his people; and like most of the Lord's anointed in ancient times, has sealed his mission and his works with his own blood; and so has his brother Hyrum" (Doctrine and Covenants 135:3).

Chapter three:

Before the seventh century, Mohammed pronounced Allah as the only one true God. Note that Allah, was the widely worshipped moon god throughout ancient Mesopotamia. This can easily be verified because Allah is found in Arabic inscriptions prior to Islam's foundation.

In order to appease the pagan populations in Arabia, Mohammed chose among the various gods, Allah, who was married to the sun goddess in their legends. (Wikipedia, Allah.) Paraphrase

The First Article of Faith:

*Article 1. We believe in God, the Eternal Father, and in His Son, Jesus Christ, and in the Holy Ghost.*

Mormons are taught that God is a glorified flesh-and-blood man who is now the God of all heaven and earth. He is said to look exactly like Jesus in appearance. Joseph Smith said:

I will go back to the beginning before the world was, to show what kind of being God is. What sort of a being was God in the beginning? ... God himself was once as we are now, and is an exalted man, ... it is necessary we should understand the character and being of God and how he came to be so; for I am going to tell you how God came to be God. We have imagined and supposed that God was God from all eternity. I will refute that idea, and take away the veil, so that you may see.... It is the first principle of the Gospel to know for a certainty the Character of God, ... and that he was once a man like us; yea, that God himself, the Father of us all, dwelt on an earth, the same as Jesus Christ himself did (Smith, *Teachings of the Prophet Joseph Smith*, p. 345).

James Talmage an early member of the quorum of the LDS twelve apostles said, "Therefore we know that both the Father and the Son are in form and stature perfect men; each of them possesses a tangible body . . . of flesh and bones" (Talmage, *Articles of Faith*, p. 38).

In a *Times Magazine* interview, August 4, 1997, Gordon B. Hinckley, the fifteenth president of the LDS church, attempted to downplay this teaching. "That gets into some pretty deep theology that we don't know very much about."

First Corinthians 8:5 says, "For though there be that are called gods, whether in heaven or in earth (as there be gods many, and lords many). Genesis 1:26 "And God said "Let us make man in our own image."

The greatest fall of all time was a result of a created being wanting to become as God.

Lucifer's fall was a result of this very idea that a created being could one day be as God or attain to the position of Godhood. Isaiah 14:12–14

How art thou fallen from heaven, O Lucifer, son of the morning! How art thou cut down to the ground, which didst weaken the nations! For thou hast said in thine heart, I will ascend into heaven, I will exalt my throne above the stars of God: I will sit also upon the mount of the congregation, in the sides of the north: I will ascend above the heights of the clouds; I will be like the most High.

In Genesis 3:5, we read how Satan's temptation to Adam and Eve related this very same desire to be as God. "For God doth know that in the day ye eat thereof, then your eyes shall be opened, and ye shall be as gods, knowing good and evil."

1 Timothy 3:16: "And *without controversy* great is *the mystery of godliness*: God was manifest in the flesh, justified in the Spirit, seen of angels, preached unto the Gentiles, believed on in the world, received up into glory"

The Bible clearly teaches that God does not have a body of flesh and blood, but is a Spirit.
John 4:23–24
Luke 24:39
1 Timothy 1:17
Numbers 23:19
The Bible teaches us God is eternal.
Psalm 41:13:
Psalm 90:2
1 Timothy 1:17
Malachi 3:6
Revelation 1:8
In Revelation 4:8, those around the heavenly throne affirm: "Holy, holy, holy, Lord God Almighty, which was, and is, and is to come." Thus our God is, always and forever, God the Eternal Father, never a mere mortal man.

The Bible teaches us there is only one God.
1 Corinthians 8:4–6
Galatians 3:20

1 Timothy 2:5
Isaiah 45:18
James 2:19

Chapter four:

Mormons are taught to believe Jesus was the first spirit to be born in heaven rather than an eternal part of the triune nature of God.

Apostle McConkie wrote, "The first spirit to be born in heaven was Jesus" (*Mormon Doctrine*, p. 129). Joseph F. Smith, sixth prophet of the LDS church said, "Among the spirit children of Elohim, the firstborn was and is Jehovah, or Jesus Christ, to whom all others are juniors" (*Gospel Doctrine*, p. 70).

Mormons are taught to believe Jesus and Satan are spirit brothers, and we were all born as siblings in heaven (*Mormon Doctrine*, p. 163; *Gospel Through the Ages*, p. 15).

Mormons are taught that the spirit of man is not created being: "The spirit of man is not a created being; it existed from eternity." History of the church, page 387 Deseret news 1905)

According to the Bible, however, man is not eternal but, like the angels, is a created being. Man's spirit came into existence when God breathed into his nostrils "the breath of life" (his spirit). At that point, man became a living soul. "And the LORD God formed man of the dust of the ground, and breathed into his nostrils the breath of life; and man became a living soul" (Genesis 3:7).

1 Corinthians 15:45–46: "And so it is written, The first man Adam was made a living soul; the last Adam was made a quickening spirit. Howbeit that was not first which is spiritual, but that which is natural; and afterward that which is spiritual

Jeremiah 1:5 are examples of God's foreknowledge, not evidence of preexistence:

According to their teachings, there was a "preexistence counsel" in heaven, wherein God asked who He would send to make atonement for the coming sins of mankind that would be inevitable. Jesus stood and said, "here am I, send me and the glory be thine forever" (Moses 4:2 D&C of the Church of the LDS Church).

Lucifer stood and offered his services but claimed he would lose none (to hell). He would do this by taking away our free-will/agency, the catch was that he wanted the glory for himself (Moses 4:1 D&C of the Church of the LDS Church)

Bruce R. McConkie, a member of the church's quorum of the twelve apostles, stated "Christ was begotten by an Immortal Father in the same way that mortal men are begotten by mortal fathers" (*Mormon Doctrine*, by Bruce McConkie, p. 547). "The birth of the Saviour was as natural as are the births of our children; it was the result of natural action. He partook of flesh and blood—was begotten of his Father, as we were of our fathers" (*Journal of Discourses*, vol. 8, p. 115). "He was not born without the aid of Man, and that Man was God." (*Doctrines of Salvation*, by Joseph Fielding Smith, 1954, 1:18).

Mormons are taught that Jesus paid for our sins in the garden of Gethsemane more so than on the cross.

Apostle Bruce McConkie stated "Where and under what circumstances was the atoning sacrifice of the Son of God made? Was it on the Cross of Calvary or in the Garden of Gethsemane? It is to the Cross of Christ that most Christians look when centering their attention upon the infinite and eternal atonement. And certainly the sacrifice of our Lord was completed when he was lifted up by men; also, that part of his life and suffering is more dramatic and, perhaps, more soul stirring. But in reality the pain and suffering, the triumph and grandeur, of the atonement took place primarily in Gethsemane" [where he bled from every pour] (*Doctrinal New Testament Commentary*, vol. 1, p. 774).

Mormon leaders such as Brigham Young taught that not all sins were paid for at the cross, but some such as murder and repeated adultery must be atoned for by the blood of the individual.

Brigham Young and other leaders whom Mormons believe to be the mouthpieces of God taught; "Jesus' sacrifice was not able to cleanse us from sins such as murder and repeated adultery."

They taught instead that a man's own blood must atone for these types of sins. Brigham Young stated the following: "If you find your brother in bed with your wife, and you put a javelin through them both, you would be justified and they would [have] atoned for their sins and be received into the kingdom of God. ... There is not a man or woman, who violates the covenants made with their God, that will not be required to pay the debt. The blood of Christ will never wipe that out, your own blood must atone for it" (*Journal of Discourses,* vol. 3, p. 247).

Jesus is the only way.

John 14:6

John 10:7–10

Matthew 24:24

Jesus was either what He claimed to be or a raving lunatic, look at what He said of Himself.

John 16:27

John 17:8

John 10:30

The Bible teaches that Jesus is the only way to God

1 John 5:12

John 5:39

The Bible teaches us Jesus is Immanuel, God with us.

Isaiah 7:14

Matthew 1:23

Isaiah 9:6

John 1:1–5

John 8:58

Exodus 3:14

John 6:62

John 1:18, no human has at any time seen God

John 14:9

Colossians 1:13–19

Colossians 2:9

Spirit of God: "God is a Spirit, and they that worship Him must worship Him in Spirit and in Truth" (John 4:24).

Hebrews 1:14 declares, "Are they not all ministering spirits, sent forth to minister for them who shall be heirs of salvation?

Psalm 104:4 and Hebrews 1:7 both say that God "maketh his angels spirits, and his ministers a flaming fire."

Lucifer

Ezekiel 28:13

Ezekiel 28:14–17: "Thou art the anointed cherub that covereth; and I have set thee so: thou wast upon the holy mountain of God; thou hast walked up and down in the midst of the stones of fire. *[See Psalm 104:4.]*

Exodus 25:22

1 Kings 8:7

Isaiah 14:12–16

The Bible teaches that Christ was born of a virgin

Isaiah 7:14

Luke 1:34

Matthew 1:25

The Holy Ghost "overshadowed" Mary; He did not "know" her

Luke 1:35

Matthew 1:18

The Engagement of Mary and Joseph.

Deuteronomy 22:23–24 tells us how serious a crime it was to have sex with a woman who was betrothed:

The Bible teaches that it was only at the cross that Jesus paid for our sins.

John 3:14

Numbers 21:9

Galatians 3:13

Hebrews 9:15

Hebrews 9: 16–17
The Bible teaches Jesus paid for all of our sins.
1 John 1:9
James 2:10–11
Romans 6:23

Mormons are taught that the Holy Ghost is a separate "personage" from God and not part of the same triune nature of God (D&C 130:22).

"burning of the bosom."

Mormon scripture: Moroni 10:4: And when ye shall receive these things, I would exhort you that ye would ask God, the Eternal Father, in the name of Christ, if these things are not true; and if ye shall ask with a sincere heart, with real intent, having faith in Christ, he will manifest the truth of it unto you, by the power of the Holy Ghost.

It is also stated in the Doctrine and Covenants of the LDS Church (D&C 9:8) "But, behold, I say unto you, that you must study it out in your mind; then you must ask me if it be right, and if it is right I will cause that your bosom shall burn within you; therefore, you shall feel that it is right."

Holy Ghost goes out from God and is God

Luke 3:22
Matthew 1:18

but unto him that blasphemeth against the Holy Ghost it shall not be forgiven" (Luke 12:10).

When Christ was on the earth, the Holy Spirit was not yet an indwelling presence because Immanuel (God Himself in Christ) was present. "But this spake he of the Spirit, which they that believe on him should receive: for the Holy Ghost was not yet given; because that Jesus was not yet glorified" (John 7:39).

He answered and said unto them, Because it is given unto you to know the mysteries of the kingdom of heaven, but to them it is not given" (Matthew 13:11).

Ephesians 1:13 explains it: "In whom ye also trusted, after that ye heard the word of truth, the gospel of your salvation: in whom also after that ye believed, ye were sealed with that holy Spirit of promise." Ephesians 4:30 further instructs that we "grieve not the holy Spirit of God, whereby ye are sealed unto the day of redemption."

Can Satan give us a feeling of peace? Matthew 7:22–23 says, "Many will say to me in that day, Lord, Lord, have we not prophesied in thy name? and in thy name have cast out devils? and in thy name done many wonderful works? And then will I profess unto them, I never knew you: depart from me, ye that work iniquity."

More on the Blasphemy against the Holy Ghost.

Hebrews 6:4–6.

God is faithful to forgive 1 John 1:9

It is the ground, or the receiver, however, that God uses to produce the fruit if we are willing Matthew 13:8

Chapter Six:

2nd Article of Faith of the Church of Jesus Christ of Latter-day Saints

*Article 2. We believe that men will be punished for their own sins, and not for Adam's transgression.*

They teach that procreation would not have been possible had they not seen the wisdom in disobeying God. This is expressed in The book of Moses {found in the LDS scripture called, the, Pearl of Great Price} 5:11: "And Eve, his wife, heard all these things and was glad, saying: Were it not for our transgression we never should have had seed, and never should have known good and evil, and the joy of our redemption, and the eternal life which God giveth unto all the obedient"

Luke 12:32. "Fear not, little flock; for it is your Father's good pleasure to give you the kingdom." It was never His desire that Adam should fall and suffer. He wanted to walk with them and bless them with everything He had created and had said was "very good" (Genesis 1:31).

He did know they would fall, however, and He prepared for that. As the Bible says, Jesus was "slain from the foundation of the world" (Luke 11:50).

Corinthians 15:39 clearly states, "All flesh is not the same flesh: but there is one kind of flesh of men, another flesh of beasts, another of fishes, and another of birds.

The Lord made us—mankind—to be free
Deuteronomy 30:19–20
Genesis 3:16–19 also makes it clear that the fall was nothing to rejoice over, but rather, a cause of great sorrow.

"Unto the woman he said, I will greatly multiply thy sorrow and thy conception; in sorrow thou shalt bring forth children; and thy desire shall be to thy husband, and he shall rule over thee. And unto Adam he said, Because thou hast hearkened unto the voice of thy wife, and hast eaten of the tree, of which I commanded thee, saying, Thou shalt not eat of it: cursed is the ground for thy sake; in sorrow shalt thou eat of it all the days of thy life; Thorns also and thistles shall it bring forth to thee; and thou shalt eat the herb of the field; In the sweat of thy face shalt thou eat bread, till thou return unto the ground; for out of it wast thou taken: for dust thou art, and unto dust shalt thou return."

The Bible does not imply Adam and Eve were unable to have children before they sinned
Genesis 1:28
God is not in the tempting business. He does not use sin to fulfill His purposes. "Let no man say when he is tempted, I am tempted of God: for God cannot be tempted with evil, neither tempteth he any man" (James 1:13

If you look closely at the genealogies stated in Genesis, it was common for people of the day to wait over a hundred years before having a first child. One example of this is found in Genesis 5:18: "And Jared lived an hundred sixty and two years, and he begat Enoch."

The Bible teaches that when Adam sinned, it not only brought physical death to all, but "spiritual death" (separation from the presence of God) for all mankind.

James 1:15
Romans 5:12
Matthew 7:17–18
Romans 8:7
Isaiah 59:2
Romans 3:10
Romans 8:20–22

If I do not repent and except Jesus as my Savior before I die, I may also be accountable for the sins of those influenced my failure to teach the truth I know.

Ezekiel 3:18
Matthew 23:35–36
The Bible teaches that the children of believers are covered
Corinthians 7:14

Chapter seven:

The Third Article of Faith of the Church of Jesus Christ of Latter-day Saints

*Article 3. We believe that through the atonement of Christ, all mankind may be saved, by obedience to the laws and ordinances of the Gospel*

In the days before Christ, God instituted a system of atonement that was a foreshadowing of the ultimate atonement of a perfect life. But it was not possible that the blood of goats and bulls could fully atone for sin.

Hebrews 9:9 says that this sacrifice "was a figure for the time then present, in which were offered both gifts and sacrifices, that could not make him that did the service perfect, as pertaining to the conscience."

Sold ourselves into sin but Jesus buys us back.

The concept of redemption comes from the law of the near-of-kin redeemer, as expressed in Leviticus 25:47–49

Romans 7:14


Job 19:25
Psalm 19:14
The ordinances were a shadow and a type of things to come.
Colossians 2:14
Colossians 2:20
Ephesians 2:15
Hebrews 9:1
Hebrews 9:10


Chapter Seven:


Only one way to God

John 14:6, "I am the way, the truth, and the life: no man cometh unto the Father, but by me."


Chapter Eight:


Receive Christ
John 3:3
John 1:12
Romans 10:9–11
by grace are ye saved through faith
Ephesians 2:8–10
John 3:16
He does the work
Hebrews 12:2
Colossians 1:22
Hebrews 12:6

James 2:12 warns us we should speak and act and live as those that will be judged by the law

How long does salvation last

Romans 8:35–39

John 10:28

John 3:14–15 Forever

Resurrection

Job 19:26

Revelation 21:8: "But the fearful, and unbelieving, and the abominable, and murderers, and whoremongers, and sorcerers, and idolaters, and all liars, shall have their part in the lake which burneth with fire and brimstone: which is the second death."

Who is a "good person"?

You may say, "I've never killed; I've never stolen," and so forth. Yet the Bible says if you are guilty of breaking just one part of the Law, just one commandment, you are guilty of breaking the whole Law. "For whosoever shall keep the whole law, and yet offend in one point, he is guilty of all. For he that said, Do not commit adultery, said also, Do not kill. Now if thou commit no adultery, yet if thou kill, thou art become a transgressor of the law" (James 2:10–11).

Matthew 19:26

Chapter Nine:

The Fourth Article of Faith of the Church of Jesus Christ of Latter-day Saints

*Article 4. We believe that the first principles and ordinances of the Gospel are: first, Faith in the Lord Jesus Christ; second, Repentance; third, Baptism by immersion for the remission of sins; fourth, Laying on of hands for the gift of the Holy Ghost.*

This they teach, despite the fact that Christ Himself did not keep others who were not apostles from taking authority to use His name. (See Mark 9:38–39.)

What the Bible teaches about the principles of the gospel; Jesus as first and last.

In Revelation 1:17

Peter 1:9

The work of God is complete in Jesus Christ. All who accept Jesus as Lord are saved. Those who are saved will receive everything God has to offer—not part, not some, but all that God has will be ours to share in His kingdom. Consider these statements:

Romans 8:32

1 Corinthians 3:21–23

2 Peter 1:3

Revelation 21:7

Things in Heaven are no more like earth than a seed looks like the wheat it produces. "And that which thou sowest, thou sowest not that body that shall be, but bare grain, it may chance of wheat, or of some other grain" (1 Corinthians 15:37).

Philippians 3:21

Matthew 22:30

Galatians

1 Corinthians 2:9

King David gave us a small picture of this kind of love as recorded in 2 Samuel 1:26

We are then pronounced just and holy, unable to be convicted of sin—unblameable. Consider this passage from Colossians 1:21–23:

if it were a "saving ordinance," there would have been no need to have been baptized more than once, as some of the follows of John were:

Acts 19:1–5

The man on the cross next to Jesus, and what he teaches us.

Luke 23:43

On the website, www.LDS.org, the following is posted:

"Baptism for the Dead. Thus, those who die without a knowledge of Christ have the opportunity to hear the glad message of redemption, exercise faith, and repent of their sins. But what of baptism? As the Lord taught Nicodemus, a person must be baptized—born of water—before he can enter the kingdom of heaven (John 3:5). Jesus himself was baptized "to fulfill all righteousness" (Matt. 3:15), and he instructed his apostles to baptize those who accepted the gospel message, telling them "He that believeth and is baptized shall be saved" (Mark 16:16). How, then, can those who died without the chance to be baptized receive this ordinance? The answer is that they can receive it vicariously. Just as Jesus performed a labor for us that we could not perform for ourselves, so can we perform the ordinance of baptism for those who have died, allowing them the opportunity to become heirs of salvation."

So what is being "born of the water

John 4:14

Ephesians 5:26

This life is the time to accept the Lord, not the hereafter

Hebrews 9:27

Hebrews 9:27

Psalm 88:10–11

Luke 16:26

No sin is held against God's elect, we are completely free of all guilt.

Romans 8:33–34

What the Bible teaches about receiving of the gift of the Holy Ghost.

Acts 10:44


Chapter Ten:


The Fifth and Sixth Articles of Faith of the Church of Jesus Christ of Latter-day Saints

*Article 5. We believe that a man must be called of God, by prophecy, and by the laying on of hands by those who are in authority, to preach the Gospel and administer in the ordinances thereof.*

*Article 6. We believe in the same organization that existed in the Primitive Church, namely, apostles, prophets, pastors, teachers, evangelists, and so forth.*

How does Christ fit into the leadership of the church in relation to Moses?

Matthew 23:2

Whereas there used to be a separation between God and man

Mark 15:38

Hebrews 9:12

Hebrews 10:10–17

The order of Melchizedek

Hebrews 5:4–6

Jesus did not take the honor of being the High Priest unto Himself, but was ordained by God. Hebrews 7:17

Done away in Christ

Hebrews 8:11

Joel 2:28–29

we who are in Christ became a nation of prophets, priests, and kings

Revelation 1:6

Matthew 20:25–28

The church of God is a people, it is in us and among us. "Neither shall they say, Lo here! or, lo there! for, behold, the kingdom of God is within you" (Luke 17:21)

Chapter Eleven:

Contrary to Mormon teachings found in The Pearl of Great Price and the Book of Mormon, the prophets of old were not given the full revelation that the Gentiles would also be equal with them. This is made clear in Ephesians 3:4–7:

Joseph Smith that are held as scripture teach that the prophets of these writings had a revelation of the preaching of the gospel to the gentiles. For instance, 1 Nephi 13:42

What about paid pastors?
Numbers 18:23–24
1 Chronicles 9:33
2 Corinthians 11:8
1 Corinthians 9:9–11
Other uses of tithe monies
Kings 12:16
We are the temple of God, we no longer need a building made with hands
1 Corinthians 3:16
Mark 14:58
1 Peter 2:5
What does the church look like now
Ephesians 4:11–13
1 Corinthians 4:16
The Bible specifically teaches that the offices of deacon and elder in the church were not for young boys of twelve to nineteen years of age as the Mormons use, but for seasoned men of understanding.
1 Timothy 3:2
1Timothy 3:8–13

Chapter Twelve:

Articles of Faith Seven through Nine of the Church of Jesus Christ of Latter-day Saints

*Article 7. We believe in the gift of tongues, prophecy, revelation, visions, healing, interpretation of tongues, and so forth.*

*Article 8. We believe the Bible to be the word of God as far as it is translated correctly; we also believe the Book of Mormon to be the word of God.*

*Article 9. We believe all that God has revealed, all that He does now reveal, and we believe that He will yet reveal many great and important things pertaining to the Kingdom of God.*

Mormon prophet's "revelation" supersedes the written word. The following is a quote from www.LDS.org on the subject:

This [Mormon] Church constantly needs the guidance of its head, the Lord and Savior, Jesus Christ. This was well taught by President George Q. Cannon, formerly a member of the First Presidency: "We have the Bible, the Book of Mormon and the Book of Doctrine and Covenants; but all these books, without the living oracles and a constant stream of revelation from the Lord, would not lead any people into the Celestial Kingdom of God. This may seem a strange declaration to make, but strange as it may sound, it is nevertheless true. "Of course, these records are all of infinite value. They cannot be too highly prized, nor can they be too closely studied. But in and of themselves, with all the light that they give, they are insufficient to guide the children of men and to lead them into the presence of God. To be thus led requires a living Priesthood and constant revelation from God to the people according to the circumstances in which they may be placed" (Gospel Truth: Discourses and Writings of President George Q. Cannon, 2 vols., sel. Jerreld L. Newquist, 1974, 1:323).

Here again is some text taken from the site www.LDS.org. With the question, then why don't they use it?

"The Joseph Smith Translation of the Bible: With the restoration of divine priesthood authority and the reestablishment of the Church of Jesus Christ through the Prophet Joseph Smith, there came also the restoration of ancient scriptures. Not only were we to have a Bible, but also a Book of Mormon and other sacred records. The revelations received by the Prophet Joseph Smith made clear that the King James Version, great as it was, did not contain all that the ancient manuscripts had once contained.

Many plain and precious things had been lost (see 1 Ne.13). It was not so much a matter of translation of languages, but also a faulty transmission of the text. The King James Version is thus a remarkable vestige of an even more remarkable record of the gospel that was preached anciently. With the Restoration, another revision of the English Bible was in order, not by a scholar but by a prophet. And it would come not from an ancient manuscript but from direct revelation of the same Lord from whom the Bible had originated. It was to be done at the Lord's commission rather than at the request of an earthly monarch or pope. This revision was to be an inspired version of the King James Bible, a divine restoration of ancient biblical knowledge. It is known today as the Inspired Version, or more properly, as the Joseph Smith Translation of the Bible. It should be seen in perspective as another step in the struggle to give mankind a Bible that not only can be read, but also can be understood. The Prophet Joseph Smith made his translation during the years 1830 to 1844."

The law came in to show us just how great our need was, and how impossible to achieve our goal by our own efforts to become holy

Romans 5:20

Romans 7:12–13

Isaiah 64:6

The apostles were then given the assignment to be the special witnesses of all that they had both seen and heard the Lord do and of His resurrection from the dead.

Acts 1:22

Luke 24:46–49

Go not into the way of the Gentiles, and into any city of the Samaritans enter ye not: but go rather to the lost sheep of the house of Israel" (Matthew 10:5–6

Matthew 28:19

All these things have an end
1 Corinthians 13:9–12

Chapter Thirteen:

*Article 10. We believe in the literal gathering of Israel and in the restoration of the Ten Tribes; that Zion (the New Jerusalem) will be built upon the American continent; that Christ will reign personally upon the earth; and that the earth will be renewed and receive its paradisiacal glory.*

*Article 11. We claim the privilege of worshiping Almighty God according to the dictates of our own conscience, and allow all men the same privilege, let them worship how, where, or what they may.*

*Article 12. We believe in being subject to kings, presidents, rulers, and magistrates, in obeying, honoring, and sustaining the law.*

*Article 13. We believe in being honest, true, chaste, benevolent, virtuous, and in doing good to all men; indeed, we may say that we follow the admonition of Paul—*

*We believe all things, we hope all things, we have endured many things, and hope to be able to endure all things. If there is anything virtuous, lovely, or of good report or praiseworthy, we seek after these things.*

Where are the lost tribes
Romans 9:6–8
Luke 17:20–21
Galatians 3:29
The whole of the covenant that God made with Abraham began with the promise of the specific land of Canaan, recorded in Genesis 17:7–9
1 Chronicles 28:8

"establishing their own righteousness." Romans 10:2–4:

Chapter Fifteen:

**Here are some key scriptures to lead one to salvation**
**Romans 3:23**—Everyone sins.
**Romans 3:10**—No one is "good."
**Romans 6:23**—We earned the death sentence.
**John 3:3**—You must be "born again."
**John 1:12**—Those who receive Him are given the power to become "sons of God."
**Romans 10:9–11**—We receive Him by a confession of faith and true belief in the heart that leads unto right living.
**2 Corinthians 5:15**—After we receive Him, our life is no longer our own. We do not have the right to live life for our own pleasure, but we live for the pleasure of God.
**Revelation 3:20**—God wants a personal, sit-down-to-a-meal-together relationship with each of us. He will not barge into our lives, however. He "stands at the door" of our hearts, knocking; we must invite Him in.

If you want to know for yourself if what I am saying is true, Seek the Lord and to know Him through His Word, as recorded in the Bible. Do this seeking with all your heart, might, mind and strength and you will find the answers for yourself. Don't put your eternal soul in the hands of mere men. Don't trust the words of a mere human to tell you what God Himself wants to reveal to you personally through a living relationship with His Word, the Bible, and by His Spirit. Even in the Christian world, there are wolves in sheep's clothing, weeds among the wheat, false leaders who care nothing for God's people, but to feed themselves and clothe themselves with the wool. (see Ezekiel 34) If you come to know the truth, you will be able to spot them easily by their fruit, not just their words.